bloom

stories to heal the mind
Jinny Tavee, M.D.

bloom

Disclaimer: The information provided in this publication contains opinions and ideas of the author, and is not intended to be a substitute for professional medical advice or instruction. Please discuss with your health care provider any matter relating to your personal health. No action should be taken based solely on the contents of this publication. Also, reading the information in this publication does not create a physician-patient relationship. The author and publisher assume no responsibility for any risk, liability, or injury resulting either directly or indirectly from the contents of this book. This publication is not responsible for errors or omissions.

First Edition
Printed in The United States by
Davis Graphic Communications Solutions
101 Robinson Ave.
Barberton, Ohio 44203

ISBN: 978-0-692-42123-9

bloom

For my mother

with much love and admiration

bloom:
stories to heal the mind

. . . .

Table of Contents

The Stories

bloom

A
collection of stories
to help us understand
to find joy
to begin again
to bloom

bloom

Not So Great Expectations

I n the face of life's uncertainties, I am sure of one thing: I will never enjoy gambling. The potential thrill of winning a small fortune is greatly outweighed by the sheer anxiety of losing even just one of my hard-earned dollars. Gambling for me is equivalent to watching my money burn. But when the lottery jackpot hit a record $600 million a few years ago, I, like everyone else in my office, bought a ticket and dreamed of quitting my job.

As the jackpot grew, advice flowed freely on what to do if we won, whether to take our winnings in lump sum or divided payments, and, of course, how to spend all that money. The beauty of it was that we all had an equal chance of winning no matter who we were or what our backgrounds happened to be. And so the general spirit was one of unity where we were all in on this collective fantasy even though the chances of winning were slim to none. It was said that a person was more likely to be attacked by a shark or hit by lightning *twice*. Most people understood this and weren't too heartbroken when a couple in Georgia ended up with the winning numbers, although there was a mild sense of disappointment in the air the day after it was announced. This is wishing, the most benign form of wanting.

It's natural to want things. Beyond the basic necessities of food, shelter and safety, it is our tendency to want the things that we see. If someone has a nice jacket that we admire, drives a fancy car that turns heads or receives a promotion at work, we can acknowledge that we like it and wish for a moment that that could be ours too. And if it's really important to us and would be a positive thing in our lives, we can work toward obtaining whatever it is that we want. Otherwise, we just have to let it go. What is more dangerous and more common, however, is expectation. This is taking wanting to another level. To borrow the metaphor used by the late meditation master, S.N. Goenka, the difference between wishing and expecting is a mark in the sand versus a mark in the stone. With one small wave of the tide the mark in the sand is gone, but it can take many years for the mark in stone to be washed away. Similarly, if we wish to win the lottery, but find that our numbers don't match the ones on the little balls that pop out of the machine, it's no big loss. It was just a "could be" that didn't happen. We get over it quickly and move on with our lives. But when we expect something, there is usually more emotional investment and often more effort involved. It's not just a "could be" anymore. When we expect something, we feel that it "should be." It's just a matter of time before it's ours. So when we don't get it, we are annoyed, indignant and angry. The amount of emotion and suffering that we feel is equal to how much we wanted it.

It's like when we've spent a good 20 minutes looking for a parking spot and finally find what we think is an open space. But when we actually try to pull in, we realize that the reason why it's still open is that the car next to it is so badly parked that it takes up half the space. Even though someone else probably would have taken that spot long before we got there had the car been parked correctly, all reason is thrown out the window when we're running late and tired of circling the parking lot. Some of us may mutter unkind words under our breath, leave nasty notes under the windshield wiper or worse. The degree of anger varies, but the feeling is the same. We expect people to park within the lines. And therein lies the problem. It's our expectation that people will follow the rules and be courteous and considerate of others that gives us grief. But the reality is that some people just do what they want to do. This is life. We can throw a self-righteous tantrum and let it ruin our day. Or we can just accept that this is the way people are and then keep driving until we find a new spot. That's it. There's no secret. We can make things easier on ourselves by changing our thought patterns — not to expect the worst of people, but to expect nothing.

When we expect civility from the people around us, we can be sorely disappointed or even hurt. We've all been taken aback by rude store clerks or customer service agents on the phone — the very people who are paid to be nice to us. It's an unpleasant experience when we're the recipient of their scorn or rudeness, but this is just the way some people are. One of my patients is a former tennis pro who played with the likes of John McEnroe and Pete Sampras many years ago. Being of African-American descent, he encountered rampant racism in what had been a Caucasian-dominated sport for many years. This was before Tiger Woods had smashed the color barrier for golf and other sports that were not known to be ethnically diverse.

Fortunately, my patient had a mentor in Arthur Ashe, the tennis legend who was the first African-American to win Wimbledon, the U.S. Open and the French Open. Although he was a superstar, Ashe was a humble and gracious man to the very end when he tragically died of AIDS at the age of 49 after receiving a blood transfusion tainted with HIV. Over the years, Ashe would give valuable advice and words of encouragement to my patient. When people would treat him poorly at the fancy country clubs where whites-only was an unwritten rule, Ashe told him to be a gentleman no matter what was said or done to him so that after he left the people there would say, "What a nice young man. We'd love to have him back." And that's exactly what he did. Sometimes, it worked and the people welcomed him when he returned for another tournament, and other times it didn't. We can't change who people are or how they think about us in a moment's time. The only thing we can do is to try to be kind or at least civil in return.

We expect things from the people that we love. We expect our spouses or significant others will love us just as much if not more, understand us, and know how to make us happy. They should listen to us when we have a bad day or at least not make things worse by criticizing us or bringing up old arguments to fight about once again. When they fall short of what we think they should be, we get upset and resentful. We may even let it affect our behavior toward them, starting a vicious cycle in which we are less than patient and understanding when we're with them. This causes them to react in the same vein, which only makes our resentment grow. It builds and builds until there's a serious blow-up about something trivial like what kind of ice cream to buy, because there's so much underneath the surface. The reality is that no one is perfect. Unless the other person is hurting us or we're just completely incompatible, we have to accept who they are and their limitations without expecting them to be everything we want them to be. Then we can take a look at ourselves and reflect on how we can be better and kinder instead of expecting these qualities from someone else.

We expect things from our children. Some of us want them to be academic superstars. A friend of mine was told as a small child that if she colored outside of the lines, Harvard wouldn't take her. My own parents told me when I was four-years-old that when I grew up I could be any kind of doctor I wanted to be. Any kind. They honestly thought they were giving me a choice (it worked out okay in the end). One of my former colleagues admitted to being the "psycho dad" at his son's baseball games many years ago. He's actually a great guy and a very caring father, but he expected his son to be the best hitter on his team and would get visibly upset if his son didn't perform well or if the coaches or umpires were making calls that weren't in his son's favor. After he was thrown out of a couple games for his disruptive behavior, he changed his ways to everyone's relief. It took some time, but he eventually learned how to be supportive from the sidelines without causing his son and everyone else great angst at his presence.

At a more basic level, we expect our children to listen to us, respect us and do what we tell them without talking back. And that's fine when we're trying to guide them and raise them to be responsible human beings, but anyone with children knows that it doesn't always go very smoothly. A friend of mine who is a single mother of two takes it to heart when her teenage son starts mouthing back to her when she tells him to take his bath or finish his chores. She works long hours every day to provide for her family and does her best to shuttle them around town to basketball, soccer and piano lessons. So when her son refuses to do as he's told, it leaves her feeling frustrated,

angry and sometimes even sad. Through trial and error and her fair
share of heartache, she learned how to step back and see him as a child
who's developing emotionally and testing boundaries instead of an
ungrateful brat who doesn't care about her feelings. She accepts that
he's an individual with his own mind and doesn't expect him to be the
perfect child, but firmly keeps him in line with love and discipline.

In some cases, the expectation is deep below the surface and
entangled with emotional scars that we can't see. One of my patients,
a middle-aged woman who'd suffered a neurologic disease a few
years back, came to our last appointment looking gaunt and haggard.
Although she had never fully recovered from the initial illness, she
was still active and relatively healthy. So when she came to see me in
clinic looking like she hadn't slept in days, it was quite a departure from
her usual self. It turned out that her mother had been diagnosed with
severe kidney failure and had been in and out of the hospital for the
last several months. Despite their stormy relationship and her mother's
longstanding favoritism of a younger sister, my patient dutifully sat at
her bedside day and night. Unfortunately, her mother who had always
been verbally abusive to her (nothing was ever good enough) was now
worse to the point that even the nurses were pulling my patient aside
and asking why her mother was so mean to her. The whole ordeal was
obviously causing my patient a great deal of mental and physical stress,
yet she remained at her mother's side adjusting her pillow, helping her
with her bedpan and bringing her water. I told her gently that although
she was doing the right thing, if she was waiting for her mother to give
her a nugget of kindness or some small gesture of appreciation, she
had to prepare herself for the possibility that it might never come. She
acknowledged that, but something deep inside of her still wanted her
mother to say thank you before she passed.

With this degree of emotional investment, the stakes are higher. Expectation mixed with a lifetime of hope and wishing may lead to a great deal of pain and disappointment if it all comes to nothing. But sometimes what we feel is beyond our control. The only thing to do in these instances is to prepare ourselves as best we can and to find other ways to fill the hole. After our appointment was over, I brought her to our procedure room where we perform EMGs, a rather painful nerve test that involves electric shocks and needles. She knew the room well as she'd undergone the procedure twice before. I told her to look up and see what she had paid for through a small donation she'd given to our clinic. There on the ceiling was a laminated picture of a sunset that I'd taken in upstate New York. It had been enlarged and then taped to the ceiling so that patients could feel relaxed or at least distracted during their procedure. "I did that?" she asked. I told her that her generosity would help relax and calm other patients so they could make it through their test. She hugged me and left the clinic knowing she had made a difference, that her contribution was recognized even if it was just by me.

Expecting the best from ourselves can push us to succeed, to win all the races, to be number one. But it can also result in stress, anxiety and a fear of being anything less than perfect. In severe cases, it can even lead to self-hatred. We've all heard stories about the prodigy athlete who burns out in the first year of playing professionally, the honor student who cuts herself or the writer who goes into a deep depression after failing to match the critical acclaim of his first novel. If we constantly expect to be at 100%, to be perfect all the time, we are bound to fail because it's not sustainable. It's okay to want to win, to work hard and to have self-discipline. But we also have to acknowledge that at the end of the day we are only human. We just do the best we can and accept the outcome whatever it may be.

The worst form of wanting is demanding. With this, it's not "could be" or "should be." Demanding is absolutely *has to be* without exception. By definition, when someone demands something, he is asking why it hasn't happened yet. Think of a rude traveler at the airport who's yelling at the ticket agent, demanding that he get a certain seat on a certain flight even if it's sold out. It's usually an ugly scene, because the attitude is ugly. When someone demands something from another person, it's a display of selfishness in which his agenda trumps everything else. Think of a time when someone demanded something from us, like a boss, a teacher or a significant other. In that particular instance, we may have had to comply without saying anything, but we weren't happy about it. And in reality, they weren't either. People who are demanding are not in an ideal state of mind. When the sense of self is so strong that its needs and desires have to be strongly projected onto other people, it is never a good situation. With demand, which is about power and control, the stakes are much higher than just plain wanting. Demanding does not just leave us worse for wear, it destroys us.

The best solution is to want as little as possible. The more we want, the more we suffer — even if all we want is a pleasant interaction with another human being. People can be rude. They can be selfish, self-centered and unkind. Sometimes it's ingrained into their personality, but other times we might just be catching them on a bad day. We don't have to expect the worst. That just makes us defensive, skittish and bitter in the end. Just expect nothing. Know that the world is not perfect. We are not perfect. But like Arthur Ashe advised, we can try to be our best regardless of how others are. And by doing so, we can make our lives just a little more peaceful.

Another Slice of Humble Pie

O f all the magazines my father had in the waiting room of his medical practice, the *National Enquirer* was by far the most popular. It was such a favorite among his patients that he kept up his subscription for nearly 20 years. But as much as people enjoy reading about the glamorous lives of movie stars, many of us genuinely like stories about celebrities who buy their kids ice cream cakes at Baskin-Robbins or wealthy CEOs who drive pick-up trucks instead of expensive sports cars.

A former U.S. Ambassador to China made headlines when he was seen at a Starbucks in Beijing, standing in a long line just like everyone else and then paying for a cup of coffee using a gift card. This is unheard of in China where diplomats and high-ranking officials rarely mix with everyday people and are often treated like royalty. On the other side of the world, the president of Uruguay drives an old Volkswagen Beetle to work and flies economy class.

Even Carlos Slim, the telecom billionaire in Mexico and one of the richest men in the world, has been known to wear suits from Sears and lives in the same house he did 40 years ago. And of course, the much-loved Pope Francis, who has always been a champion of the poor, rode the city bus, cooked his own meals and lived in a simple apartment when he was the archbishop of Buenos Aires. Today he lives in the visitors' guesthouse in the Vatican instead of the palatial suite that is bestowed upon the most powerful religious figure in the world.

What is it about these stories that catch our attention? Why do they touch us so much more than hearing about a pop star who wears $10,000 boots? Because it makes us feel connected with these people that we've always considered far removed from us. When we learn about how they chose to live simply at least for one aspect of their lives, we think of them as human beings — people just like us, unseparated by class or race or power. On a deeper level, we like these stories because they don't make us feel small or inadequate. In fact, they reduce our sense of self and our natural tendency toward desire and envy even if just for a moment. This is the power of humility.

At its core, humility is a state of being that's free of ego and personal gain. It's the acknowledgment that we are all a part of something bigger than ourselves and that our individual agendas are not at the center of the universe. It doesn't mean that our needs are unimportant or that we should let everyone walk all over us. Nor does it imply that we're invisible wallflowers who constantly need to put ourselves down. We can still excel and achieve great things, but we can do this without a sense of self-importance. In his online article on humility in the running world where fierce competition and petty rivalries are widespread, the journalist David Alm wrote about his brief experience with elite African runners.[1] Instead of the cutting remarks that his fellow American runners would sometimes make if his times were just slightly slower than theirs in local races, the runners from Kenya, who are well known to be among the fastest in the world, gave him words of support and encouragement during their workouts together. They were inclusive and generous in spirit despite their domination of the sport and an almost perpetual spot in the winners' circle at every major race. He describes it as a different attitude, a general feeling of community that allowed these world-class runners to treat others not as competitors or slower runners to be dismissed, but simply as human beings.

While humility is in reality a state of mind, we can certainly try to speak and carry ourselves in a modest fashion. The appearance of modesty can be an outward expression of humility, but only if it's in sync with how we truly think and feel. If behind those self-deprecating comments, there is an air of self-righteousness or a hidden agenda (e.g., fishing for compliments), then what we're left with is false modesty. It's like when we see a serial killer in court who's dressed conservatively and has been trained by the defense lawyer to keep his head down in order to earn sympathy from the jurors. It's all just an act that means absolutely nothing if he feels no guilt or remorse for his crimes.

When we think of people we know who aren't humble, we can recall how it's very hard to be around them sometimes. People who are egotistical and unable to yield to others are unknowingly harsh in their personal interactions. They are overbearing and unconcerned with the needs of others, always having to do things their way. As time passes, their sense of self and ego accumulate. They don't care about anyone else but themselves. They become hardened in their never-ending battle to preserve their inflated egos and will never truly be happy. In the end, they suffer greatly and so do the people in their lives.

In contrast, people who are humble are often wonderful to be with. During my internship, I had the privilege of rotating with an infectious disease specialist who is one of the kindest people I've ever met. When I first saw her in the audience at a medical lecture many years ago, I thought she was just another resident physician. But then the lecturer, who was presenting a difficult case, stopped to ask her what kind of infection the patient could have had. In a gentle but very clear voice, she rattled off a list of bacteria and viruses that I've never even heard of. Without an ounce of pretension, she went on to describe what parts of the world they could be found in, symptoms the patients would present with and how to make the diagnosis for each bug. I was blown away. I later learned she was educated wholly through the Harvard system for her undergraduate studies, medical school and training. Yet, she never brought this up in conversation like some people do to impress others. She had even taught herself several languages and knew more Thai than I did.

Working with her for a month, I saw how she treated all of her patients with the same amount of compassion regardless of whether they were homeless drug abusers or a wealthy VIP. In medical conferences, where many physicians like to stand out as the smartest person in the room, she would simply state her opinion without being pompous or condescending. If someone disagreed with her, she was never confrontational. She would say that the other person had an interesting point and that he or she might be right. She never tried to show everyone how smart she was and didn't care about looking good in front of others. She was just a brilliant, kind and hardworking physician, and everyone knew it. One of the pharmacists who was making rounds with us one day joked that she had a one-way express ticket to heaven with no stops.

In everyday life, there are opportunities for us to be more humble starting with how we interact with other people. When we're in a conversation we can listen more to the other person instead of thinking about what we're going to say next or focusing on trying to get our point across. When we give someone our full attention and let the other person do most of the talking, it makes him feel important and in turn reduces our ego and sense of self. Afterwards, the other person will walk away with a positive feeling not only about the conversation but also about us, even if we said very little. Also, when we're in the middle of a discussion with someone, we can keep in mind the two magic words of a successful marriage: "yes, dear." It's not really the words, but the philosophy of it. In most cases, we can use a variation, like "You may be right." It seems trite, but it really does work to lessen our pride and it definitely keeps the peace. And if for some reason, we just don't agree with the other person, then we can acknowledge her opinion and say, "That's an interesting perspective" or "I see your point" and leave it at that instead of reiterating our own argument.

In the setting of an everyday conversation, it's not a matter of winning or losing. When we tell another person that she may be right, it's an open recognition that we don't know everything and that we could be wrong. More importantly, it's showing the other person that we respect her and her ideas regardless of whether or not we agree with her. The late scientist Carl Sagan said, "In science it often happens that scientists say, 'You know that's a really good argument; my position is mistaken,' and then they would actually change their minds and you never hear that old view from them again. They really do it. It doesn't happen as often as it should, because scientists are human and change is sometimes painful. But it happens every day. I cannot recall the last time something like that happened in politics or religion."

Another way we can be more humble is to share the limelight and give credit to others when we are recognized for something, like a star athlete who acknowledges the contributions of his teammates even if his performance single-handedly won the game. A family friend of mine who is a dentist in solo practice gives all of her office employees a large bonus at the end of the month whenever her practice does well. Although patients obviously come for her expertise, she realizes that she can't provide the excellent level of care she does without the efficiency of her staff and the warm atmosphere they generate. Even if we accomplish something solely as an individual, we can still show humility by being grateful toward the people who supported us or somehow made it possible for us to be in that situation. Abraham Lincoln, one of the greatest American presidents, said "All that I am or ever hope to be, I owe to my angel mother."

In the same vein, when things don't go well, we should accept responsibility for our actions without blaming others or pulling in anyone else with us. Trying to hide things or getting defensive usually just makes things worse. On the other hand, owning up to our mistakes keeps us grounded and our egos in check. If we do something wrong or hurt someone else, we should apologize, fix the problem if we can and then try not to do it again. When the online shoe and clothing store Zappos lost $1.6 million within six hours due to a pricing error, the CEO and founder Tony Hsieh, who has made "Be humble" one of the company's core principles, accepted sole responsibility for the mistake, fired no one and honored all of the customer sales during that time period even though a legal stipulation on their website said they didn't have to.

We can also work on our humility by learning how to accept compliments and positive feedback in a graceful but neutral manner. Of course, it's natural to feel happy when someone tells us how great we are, especially when we did something rather routine that we didn't think was deserving of such praise. But if we allow ourselves to float up into the clouds whenever we are told that we're wonderful, then we start to feed off of it or crave it. We may even need a constant supply to maintain our self-esteem. To make matters worse, if we allow the good comments to go to our heads and puff out our chests, then the flipside is that a negative comment or criticism will bring us crashing down. Any time we let our sense of self-worth be dependent on how others see us, we put ourselves on an emotional rollercoaster that can fluctuate from minute to minute. Just recently, a patient I had seen was unsatisfied with me and called the clinic to switch to another physician. Within a few hours, I received an email from another patient who thanked me profusely for the care I had given him. I provided the same level of service for both patients and yet they had drastically different opinions of me as a physician. It just goes to show that it doesn't matter what other people think about us as long as we always do our best and try to do the right thing. The late Mother Teresa said, "if you are humble nothing will touch you, neither praise nor disgrace, because you know what you are."

I had a more extended and rather painful lesson about this when I asked the universe for an opportunity to learn about humility. For two weeks straight while rotating on the inpatient hospital service, I was either yelled at or talked down to by patients, their families, other staff physicians, and even physicians-in-training on a daily basis. On the last day of my rotation, I was relieved that I had made it to 6pm without a single negative comment. But on my way to see the last new patient of the day, my intern warned me that there had been a miscommunication between him and the patient, a frail woman with an aggressive cancer. To this day, I don't know exactly what was said, but the end result was that the poor patient had phoned her husband on his way home from the hospital and told him that the neurology team had just called her a junkie for being on narcotics.

I took a deep breath as I walked into her room. She was on the phone with her husband who was talking so loudly I could hear him from the doorway. I hadn't even introduced myself to her yet when the patient handed me the phone and mouthed, "I'm sorry." Before I had a chance to explain the situation, the husband shouted into the phone that he was turning the car around and coming right back to the hospital to give me a piece of his mind. After he slammed the phone down in my ear, I told the intern to go home for the day and to be more careful when he spoke to patients. Then I went downstairs and prayed as hard as I could to anyone who would listen that if I had learned enough about humility then just please lessen the verbal thrashing I was about to receive. In this case, it really was just a misunderstanding and I had done nothing wrong. But if there was still more for me to learn, then so be it. I resigned myself to the reality that if he chose to be angry and yell at me, there was nothing I could do except to remain calm and explain the situation without being angry or indignant for his misdirected rage. And so I waited for the boom to fall.

A half hour later, the nurses called me back up to the floor. When I got to the room, the husband was sitting in a chair beside the patient's bed holding her hand. The drive had calmed him down enough that she was able to explain things before I got there and everything turned out fine in the end. But even if he had screamed at me and called me every unpleasant name in the book, I would have been okay — not great, but okay — because I had made it a point to not let his opinion of me influence how I felt and behaved.

Finally, one of the best things we can do to be more humble is to stop comparing ourselves to others. Whether it's owning the biggest house in the neighborhood, having the most talented kid or being more successful than our friends, when we feel that we're in constant competition with the people around us it only breeds unhealthy thoughts. This is especially true when we think that someone is better than we are, which can make us feel jealous and inferior. We may compensate by consciously or subconsciously doing something that will make us stand out or look good in front of others. But instead of making us feel better about ourselves, it just makes the ego more fragile, and we have to do more to pump ourselves up the next time we feel inadequate. Or we may start to feel depressed about all the things that we don't have instead of feeling fortunate for all the good things in our lives. Up and down, our entire thought patterns can change depending on how we feel in relation to other people. And at the end of the day, it just makes us more self-centered because everything is all about us - how we think, how we feel. This is the opposite of humility. The truth of the situation is that these little competitions, real or imagined, are pointless. Having the most money or most prestige does not equate to being the happiest person. Even if someone seems to have it all — the perfect family, a successful career, love and admiration from scores of people — we will never know what's going on that person's mind. And in the end it really doesn't matter.

A dear friend and colleague was telling me about how one of his college classmates was now a billionaire who had his own investment fund and was giving financial advice to the White House. My friend joked about how his classmate was such a nice guy with a great family, and that there was nothing he could find to hate about him. He was laughing when he told me this, but in a way that suggested he felt a bit small in comparison. In reality, my friend is a fantastic physician who is nationally known in academic circles and has written countless medical textbooks and articles. He also has a loving wife and family as well as many friends who genuinely care for him. There was absolutely no reason for him to compare himself to a former classmate who had taken a completely different route in life. And yet he did, which made him feel down about himself despite all of his accomplishments. So I told him that he doesn't really know what kind of person his classmate is in a business setting nor will he ever be privy to what goes on in those boardrooms at that level of the game. But as a physician taking care of patients, my friend does his best every day to help people who are sick. He enjoys his work, and he's great at it. This is his journey, and it's really the only one he needs to worry about. When he was able to see things from that perspective, he could better appreciate all the wonderful things in his own life without trying to measure it against that of someone else.

The key to being humble is to know and understand that each of us has his or her own individual journey in life. If we just focus on what we're supposed to be doing and try to be a better person for ourselves and those around us, then little by little we will find that it doesn't matter what other people think of us. We will worry less about keeping up outward appearances or trying to prove anything to anyone. Eventually, we'll get to a point where we are comfortable and confident with who we are, which brings with it a peace of mind that is worth so much more than being number one. It's absolutely priceless.

Clueless in Kitchenware

T he clerk at the store was yelling at me. Loudly. For some reason, she had chosen not to enter the aisle where I was searching for kitchen aprons and was trying to direct me (from over 20 feet away) to where they were hanging. But despite her raised voice and wildly pointing finger, I kept walking past them. Back and forth, I would look toward the wrong side of the aisle or reach below or just above where the brightly colored aprons hung right in front of me. Exasperated, she stormed down the aisle and without hiding her irritation, she barked, "It's right there. Jeez Louise!" I happily picked up the apron and thanked her. But she had already turned her back to me and was off to charm the next customer.

As a wise man once said, we must be like the earth. Whether it's rain, snow or garbage, the earth accepts all of it equally into the ground without discrimination. Likewise, whether someone is telling me how wonderful how I am or showing their annoyance at my lack of situational awareness, I am learning to hear whatever they say simply as words — words with no connotation, no emotional impact on my being. Regardless of who we are or what we've done, not everyone is going to be a fan. We can't make everyone happy all of the time, nor is it our personal responsibility to do so. People are going to be people. Everyone has his or her own issues. If we are doing our best and someone gives us grief, that's his problem not ours. The late meditation master Ajahn Chah said, "If someone calls you a dog, look behind you and see if you have a tail. If you don't have a tail then there is no problem."

It's understandable that we should learn how to take insults with a grain of salt and not break down into an emotional mess when someone thinks we're not as clever as we'd hoped. But what do we do with the compliments, the words of praise that pump us up a bit and boost our confidence levels? Why can't we take pleasure in them? The reason is that we can't have one without the other. When we see the world in different poles and split things into opposites, we are welcoming both ends of the spectrum. They always come hand in hand. Yet, when we are able to give both ends up — neither craving praise nor avoiding criticism — something strange happens. Even though we don't have that temporary high from being told that we're the greatest thing since sliced bread, there is a different and more lasting kind of joy. It's a sense of lightness and peace that becomes internally pervasive. Over time, it spills over into all states of mind until we are able to accept things and people just as they are. Even sales clerks who would rather be elsewhere than helping clueless people find aprons.

Awake

The first time I saw dark circles under my eyes, I was sure it was just makeup that had smeared. After several attempts to wipe off the phantom mascara, I came to the realization that I just needed more sleep. Like many people, whenever I am deeply stressed or dwelling on something, I will toss and turn in bed for hours, thinking, worrying and imagining elaborate scenarios that raise my blood pressure and keep me wide awake. On one such night, I was finally able to fall asleep at about 2am when I suddenly had an epiphany in the form of severe, disabling pain in my hands that caused me to sit straight up in bed. I've had joint problems for many years that can sometimes be rather painful, but this was the worst I'd ever experienced. In my brief, somewhat confused state of agony, I let go of all the stress and fear and worry. And I remember saying to myself, "That's it. I don't want anything else from this world. I'm done. I've had it. I don't care about anything any more. Whatever happens, happens."

This was suffering, the kind that makes people ready to walk away from the material world, the one where we've lulled ourselves into thinking that it's okay to be constantly up and down depending on our circumstances. That "it's just life" when we bounce around among variations of happiness, boredom, anger, sadness and all the rest of our emotions. With my hands curled in front of me, I was done with all that. More than anything else, I just wanted peace. I was ready to shave my head and enter a monastery if the pain would just go away.

Over the next few days, I pondered why it was that extreme suffering makes us think like that, makes us ready to leave the conventional world and transcend above all material things no matter what the cost.

I think the answer is that it wakes us up from the illusion of life. It jolts us from our complacency in accepting what we think is normal — that the status quo of wanting this but not wanting that is just fine, when in fact it's not fine. It's actually the cause of our suffering. We are stuck in this never-ending dream, and a not-so-very pleasant one at that. We are constantly wanting and searching for fulfillment all around us. We look toward material comforts and social connections: money, success, marriage, children and a healthy network of friends. And yet, we don't find true and everlasting fulfillment there either.

Suffering is that blast of cold wind or a kick in the pants that shakes us from our sleep. Of course, when the suffering subsides or goes away, we drift back into our stuporous existence, not seeing the truth, the reality of all things - as I did when the pain in my hands started to fade. After it was gone, I simply fell asleep again. In every sense of the word.

Can You Cry Like This?

My sister-in-law's earliest memory is that of throwing a temper tantrum at the tender age of 3. She remembers walking around the house one morning crying at the top of her lungs for no particular reason except that she just felt like it. When she reached her parents' bathroom, she saw her father standing up at the sink and shaving in front of the mirror. He had white foam all over his face and was trying to get ready for work against the background noise of his wailing child. Rubbing her eyes with her fists she continued her little show for him, pausing now and again to take a deep breath.

When her father saw that she wasn't going to leave any time soon, he stopped shaving and calmly put his razor down at the edge of the sink. He then turned to her and said, "If you're going to cry, can you cry like this?" He put his fists up to his eyes, opened his mouth wide and then mimicked her crying but without any sound.

He even rubbed his eyes and moved his head back and forth as she had been doing, but again in complete silence. Having made his point, he then turned back to the mirror, picked up his razor and resumed shaving without giving her a second glance. Stunned by his reaction, she stopped and stared at her father who now seemed completely oblivious to her presence. After a few moments, she quietly left the room dazed and dry-eyed.

Our minds are often like this crying child. Sometimes, out of the blue we'll start thinking about things like an unresolved issue or a painful memory that we've kept in the back of our minds. One thought leads to another, and before we know it we're reliving a heated argument or worrying about things not turning out the way we want them to. All the while, we're adding new layers of thought and emotional baggage to what was already there, adding more fuel to the fire until we are completely caught in a vicious cycle of thoughts with no solution. During the day we can sometimes repress them or force them to stop by sheer willpower when we're busy and have many things to do. But when everything is quiet, when we're lying in bed at night, our thoughts come back with a vengeance. They keep us awake staring at the ceiling with occasional glances at the clock that make us even more stressed because it's 3am and we have to work the next day. And yet, we keep thinking until we finally fall asleep out of complete mental and physical exhaustion.

In these situations, the best thing we can do is to resolve things once and for all so that it is no longer an issue. True resolution, however, often requires deep insight, emotional support and sometimes even counseling — none of which is easy to come by in the wee hours of the morning. But what we can do is establish a concluding thought to serve as a temporary brake. For instance, when we're waiting for something, like an examination score, blood test results, an upcoming promotion at work or whether or not someone is going to call, our thoughts often run wild. We drive ourselves mad going through scenarios about what will happen to us if things don't turn out well. We think about all the things we could or should have done, little things that could have made a difference, and then we berate ourselves for having said this or done that. But even if we think positively and imagine that things do happen in our favor, we take it a step further and daydream about all the wonderful things we're going to do when we get what we want, or worry that it's not going to last or won't be as great as we had hoped it would be. This is where the concluding thought comes in handy. The bottom line for all of these situations is the same: at this point in time, the outcome is beyond our control. What's done is done, and we'll just deal with whatever happens, come what may. That's it — short and sweet. If we consistently tell ourselves this (sometimes out loud) over and over again every time those thoughts come into our heads, we can bring this mantra-like saying up and then break the chain of thoughts. It doesn't stop them from coming back, but the sooner we can remember that concluding thought, the faster we can make things go away until we have the resources to come up with a more definitive resolution.

Another option is to do what my sister-in-law's father did: instead of trying to think things through, which sometimes just makes everything worse, we can simply acknowledge that the mind will not shut up. We can then say to ourselves, "Okay, you want to think, then go ahead and think. Think and fantasize and worry to your heart's content, but I'm just going to sit back and watch." The minute we get out of our heads and become an objective observer, we start to see the thoughts as something separate from us like an unwanted visitor. And then something interesting happens. The thoughts just stop, like my sister-in-law when her father turned back to the mirror. He didn't yell at her to be quiet or punish her. He acknowledged her presence and said to go ahead and cry all she wanted, but without sound. Similarly, when we step outside of ourselves and just watch our thoughts without trying to repress them or add anything on, we're effectively deflating them by remaining disinterested and not giving them any further attention.

This is actually the basis for a coping strategy for anxiety that's taught by one of the neuropsychologists at the Cleveland Clinic. He tells his patients with anxiety to set aside five minutes each day to worry. Any other time during the day when they feel anxious, they are to stop immediately and remind themselves that they will have to save it for their specified time, which is usually set at the end of the day. One of his patients is a good friend of mine that I'd referred to him for help with chronic anxiety. She's a working mother of two small children who is constantly dealing with a multitude of problems such as marital stress over differences in parenting, paying the bills and having to entertain the kids on the weekends nonstop. She tells me how hard it is to raise a family, be a good wife and work full time, especially when she has her own issues from childhood that are still not completely resolved. She once tried to explain things to her mother, who couldn't understand why she felt so anxious when she had a great husband, two beautiful healthy children and a solid career. What she told her mother was that it wasn't anything external — it was all internal. The triggers all came from inside.

After her visit with the neuropsychologist, she followed his advice and would try to stop herself mid-thought during the day if she started feeling anxious. Then every evening at 6:30, she would intentionally bring up all the fear and anxiety she'd held onto during the day and then just watch everything play out without worrying about letting her daughter take a nap too late in the afternoon or trying to analyze why her husband had said this or that to her. When the timer went off at the five-minute mark, she would shut off all her thoughts and continue on with her daily routine. After doing this a few times, she started to realize how ridiculous some of her thoughts were, that they were really nonissues that she had just made into something bigger in her mind. Within a week or two, her anxiety had markedly improved and when the set time to worry came about, she wouldn't use up the whole five minutes and sometimes even skipped it because she felt fine. Eventually she reached a place where she felt healthy and balanced, and no longer needed to do the exercises anymore. She said that it was like taking a magic pill — poof, and it was all gone.

What she didn't realize at the time was that she was practicing a primitive form of mindfulness. She was observing her thoughts from a neutral position and then letting them go. This is the way we can stop the racing thoughts, the ones that cause us grief, insomnia and chronic health issues. And with continued and dedicated practice, insight will come, the kind that allows us to understand our issues and resolve them so that we can all reach a state of health and balance no matter what comes our way — even if it's a furious 3-year-old in the middle of a full-on tantrum.

bloom

Thanks for the Ramen

On Saturday afternoons throughout our childhood, my brother and I would tell our mother that she was the best cook in the world whenever she made us our favorite meal: ramen noodles with hot dog slices. For years, we believed that my mother was so happy to have us running and screaming around the house on the weekends that she went to all the trouble of making us this special treat. Little did we know that she was just too exhausted to do anything else after another crazy week of chauffeuring us to piano lessons and swim meets, helping my father with his medical practice, running errands around town, making us dinner and then cleaning the house. By the time Saturday came along, it was all she could do to throw a packet of instant ramen into some boiling water to feed her children. But despite our lunch's lack of nutritional content, we were actually very happy and grateful for the steaming bowl of noodles and little red bits of mystery meat that floated throughout the MSG-laden soup. We couldn't have asked for anything more. And that's one of life's little secrets: happiness is when you're grateful for what you have right now.

In that moment, when we are truly thankful for something, we are at peace. There is nothing more that we want. That constant internal chatter that says, "I want this, but not that," finally takes a break and we forget about our desires at least for a while. Like a bucket of water on a raging fire, being grateful temporarily reduces the heat where we can just be with the present instead of thinking about the past or worrying about the future. It's a feeling that we're okay with things just as they are. For many of us, that feeling doesn't come often enough as we tend to take things for granted and focus on all the things that we don't have.

Yes, we may be having some health issues, marital problems, financial strains or stress at work or school. But that's life. That's the real world. Everyone is going through something. In those times when we feel unhappy because we don't have this or that in our lives, that's when being grateful is even more important. At its most basic level, gratefulness is an understanding that we are not the alternative. We are not the homeless man looking for a garbage bag to keep us warm on a cold winter's night. We are not one of those starving kids in Africa that our mother reminded us about when we didn't finish our supper. And of course, there are much worse situations.

I recently saw a patient in clinic who looked like the quintessential soccer mom from an upscale suburb. She was pleasant while we chatted, but when she brought up the topic of her son, she became very sad. She recounted how he had been in a serious car accident at the age of 13 and since then he needed to be monitored at all times due to severe brain damage. Although he was now 17 and could walk and talk, he had the IQ of a 5-year-old. The accident had left him with blindness in one eye, severe hormonal problems and facial deformities. Even after several corrective surgeries, he still needed more reconstruction on his skull as his forehead kept sinking in. I told her that at least he was alive. She said, "That's what I used to tell myself whenever I felt down about everything, but it doesn't seem to work as much anymore." She looked down at the ground for a few moments trying to hold back her tears.

When she lifted her head again, she smiled softly and said that she was starting to see things in a different light after she'd watched a documentary on television about sex trafficking. According to the documentary, women from various parts of Asia were tricked into coming to the U.S. under the pretense of working in a restaurant, but instead were forced into prostitution. Once in the U.S., they were locked up during the day and never allowed to go out. They were regularly raped and abused in every way imaginable. If any of them tried to escape, their family members in Asia would be beaten and then photographed so that the women would see the results of their actions. My patient was struck by one particular girl in the film who said she wished the next man that she was forced to "entertain" would just kill her.

When my patient saw this, she told me that she suddenly realized how we live like kings and queens here, that we don't know how lucky we really are. Before the movie was over, she had her checkbook out and was just waiting for the contact information at the end of the film so that she could send in a donation. I told her that this was the American way of solving all of society's ills — writing a big fat check. We both laughed. But in truth, the memory of this documentary was what she needed to help her get through her own difficult period. It was a reminder for her to be grateful for what she did have in her life: security, safety and much love for her son. If Woody Allen was correct in his observation that life is either miserable or horrible, most of us would take miserable any day of the week and be thankful for it.[2]

Being grateful that we are not the alternative helps us appreciate what we have, although it's often just a fleeting thought. Because even though we may feel genuinely sorry for other people when we hear about their suffering, it doesn't really make a lasting effect on us because of the very fact that the suffering is happening to *other people* — people who are far away or who have no bearing on our lives. In his book *How to Win Friends and Influence People*, Dale Carnegie writes how we can be told that a million people in another country starved to death due to a terrible famine, but we'll care more about our toothache or a pain in our neck.[3] Whether it's a story we read in the papers or a dear friend who shares her pain about losing a parent, in order for something to make us feel truly grateful for what we have, we need to change the way we think. Otherwise, the story quickly leaves our mind and the focus of our attention is turned back onto ourselves.

Sometimes it takes a near catastrophic event in our own lives to make us feel grateful. The other day, one of my patients in clinic apologized for missing his follow-up appointment with me a few months earlier. He told me that his house had been hit by lightning and that they were still dealing with all the smoke and water damage. When I told them how sorry I was for their misfortune, his wife said that on the contrary they were extremely lucky. Surprised, I asked how that could be. She told me that both she and her husband have sleep apnea and wear oxygen masks at night, which are hooked up to an electrical machine that's plugged into the outlet. This in itself could have been disastrous as they could have been seriously burned or even electrocuted. Not only that, they were both sound asleep when the lightning struck their house starting a fire on the first floor. Had the wife not suddenly woken up they may not have gotten out in time. For some reason, she just sat straight up in bed at 4am and took off her mask. There was a rumbling sound of thunder in the background and a few streaks of lightning outside the window, but she didn't smell any smoke or notice anything unusual. She just had this feeling that they had been hit.

She immediately woke her husband and made him take off his mask. "I think we've been hit by lightning," she told him. He lifted his head from under the covers and took a whiff of the air. When he didn't smell anything, he went back under the blankets until his wife pushed him out of bed to go check everything out. As soon as he opened the door he saw smoke coming up the stairs to their second floor bedroom. Within minutes, they were able to grab a few things and run out of the house. Despite losing almost everything in the fire they felt incredibly grateful that they were able to escape unharmed. This gave them the strength to live out of a suitcase for several months, make daily phone calls to the insurance company and deal with a parade of contractors trying to rebuild their home. It's not how they had imagined their summer, but they're doing okay and continue to have a positive attitude.

On the flipside, when people are ungrateful and dissatisfied with life, they constantly look outside of themselves for something to please them. They are often harsh, demanding and only know how to take. And even if they get what they want, it's never enough. It doesn't matter how much money they have or how many people love and care about them, they only want more. In many ways, they are the hungry ghosts of ancient folklore. According to Buddhist and Hindu texts, a hungry ghost is a being with a giant stomach but a tiny mouth no bigger than the size of a pin. Their appetites are endless, but they will never be able to satisfy their hunger because their mouths are so small. They have been associated with drug addiction, selfishness and insatiable desires. Those who are like hungry ghosts live in their own private hell.

Although we may know people like that or even touch on it ourselves in varying degrees, we don't have to be like that. We can choose to be different, to stop wanting more and to be grateful for what we have at this very minute. It can be as simple as thinking of a time when someone did something nice for us no matter how trivial it might have been. I remember walking in the park one morning and feeling a little sad for some reason. I was completely lost in my own thoughts when a man walking his dog stopped to wish me good morning. He made empty chitchat about the weather and then we parted ways, but he smiled so kindly that it touched me and immediately brightened my morning. To this day the memory of how he was able to lift my spirits when I really needed it still brings me a sense of happiness and gratitude that he was in my life even if it was just for a moment.

But even those of us who feel that we did everything on our own or that no one ever helped us can at least be grateful to nature. On a hot summer day, we can feel grateful for a cool breeze or the shade of a tree. When we've had a long day at work and our bodies are tired or sore, we can be grateful for a hot shower and a warm bed. A year ago, I started doing a gratitude exercise before every meal. This is a common practice among many different faiths, but giving thanks for a meal can be completely nondenominational. It's a matter of thinking well of the hands that brought the food to our table. It can be the farmers who harvested the crops, the checkout girl at the grocery store, the person that cooked it, or even the chicken or plant that gave its life for us. We can learn how to be grateful by just acknowledging that someone or something made this meal possible for us. This can be expanded to include the people that we are grateful for having in our lives, like our family and friends, and wishing them all well and safe from harm. It takes but a minute or two, and yet if we do it regularly and we mean it, it has the power to soften the heart and warm the soul.

Perhaps the deepest reason why gratitude is so essential to our well-being is that it reduces our sense of self. When we are able to acknowledge that someone or something has helped us or at least paved the way, it gives us a sense of humility. It brings down the walls we built to protect ourselves from getting hurt, but that in turn isolated us. When we are grateful, it makes us feel that we are not alone, that we are connected and part of something bigger than ourselves. And so when something good happens to us, we can be appreciative and attribute it to divine grace, the alignment of the stars, the universe smiling upon us or the advice our grandmother gave us when we were little. We can always ask for more, but it's infinitely better when we can say we have enough, when we can accept our present lot with kindness for ourselves and those around us. As Meister Eckhart, a 13th century German theologian, wrote, "If the only prayer you said was thank you, it would be enough."

bloom

The Markup

n the busy street markets of Bangkok where the unmistakable smells of dried fish and exotic fruit intertwine, my relatives have forbidden me to speak. I am allowed to point at the things that I want and nod or shake my head, but I am not to say a word until the shopping transaction is complete and we are walking away with our goods in tow. This is because a foreign face or accent, especially an American one, is equated with a rich customer or one who is willing to pay more for a bag of mangoes or beaded trinkets. As soon as I start speaking in English or very broken Thai, the jig is up and the vendor immediately doubles or triples the price of his wares. And as most people know, haggling at the market is a rough sport best played by locals.

When the markup is on food and cheap souvenirs, the additional cost is usually just a few dollars. When it's on furniture or cars, it can be thousands of dollars. But the most expensive markup is the one we impose on ourselves with our own thoughts. Everything we do, all the interactions we have with other people, the world around us and even ourselves, is accompanied by an internal commentary. We have the ability to add this extra layer of thought beyond the mental action required to complete even the simplest of tasks, drawing from our past experiences and reacting to whatever it is that we're doing with a habitual response that can be one of anger, fear, anxiety or any other emotion. We make interactions that much more complex, more "expensive" than they really are.

This was illustrated by one of my patients who in a moment of frustration gave me unsolicited advice on children: don't have any. Her 12-year-old son had been giving her grief as of late and was talking back to her when he was asked to do chores. He would loudly grumble about what a pain it was to have to stop what he was doing (watching TV or playing video games) to take out the trash, and then would only do so after a yelling match with his mother that included several threats of being grounded for life. One day my patient's sister happened to be visiting and saw this daily production over the garbage play out between my patient and her son. After the exchange had gone on for a few minutes, the patient's sister whispered to her nephew that if he had to do the chores anyway, it would be less painful if he just did it without making such a fuss about it. The next day, he actually took out the trash when he was told to without saying a word. He was surprised at how easy it was and told his mother, "Wow, it's a lot faster when I just do it and not complain about it." It's almost hit-you-over-the-head simple (and I'm sure that's what his mother wanted to do sometimes), but quite profound when we apply it to our own lives.

We all have menial tasks that we must do, such as household chores, paying the bills and running to the post office. They're perfunctory, time-consuming and of no special consequence except that their completion is necessary for us to maintain our day-to-day lifestyle. We can fret and worry about them. We can dread, postpone, and begrudgingly carry them out while complaining about it every second of the way. Or we can simply do them without adding the emotional price tag of misery or boredom. It really is amazing what we can accomplish when we just shut off that internal commentary and finish a task. But it's equally amazing that the mind can make a task so miserable if we allow it to.

Everyone carries emotional baggage — some more than others. But we also create intellectual baggage by performing a complex series of mental gymnastics for what should be a simple task, for example, wanting to exercise after work. Instead of just saying to ourselves, "I'm going to the gym," we debate whether or not we should just go home and relax. Then we think about having to drive to the gym in rush hour, how long we need to work out and what time we will get home. We add another layer of thought when we worry that we won't burn enough calories if we don't work out for 30 minutes or leave out some cardio. This is followed by the fear that we'll never be able to lose any weight, which causes us to feel bad about our bodies and our overall lifestyle. Instead of just following through with our initial decision to go to the gym after work, our string of thoughts leads us to feelings of anxiety, guilt and maybe even a little depression. This is how intellectual baggage — indecision, internal debate and pathologic planning — can lead to emotional baggage.

Intellectual baggage can also be created out of something that's not a concrete choice or a yes-no issue. In fact, it can be created out of nothing at all. One of the clinic nurses once told me how she received a voicemail that kept her up all night and put her in an emotional storm. Someone at the blood bank where she regularly gives blood left a message on her voicemail asking her to call back as soon as she could to talk about her recent donation. Panicked, she called several times that evening but was not able to get through before the blood bank closed. That night she thought of all the terrible things that they could have found in her blood. As a health care worker, she was constantly exposed to infections like HIV and hepatitis C, which are very contagious. She was also concerned about the possibility that they had found leukemia or any other kind of blood cancer, especially as she had once worked in an oncology clinic. Her fear grew exponentially with each new disease that came into her mind. She worried about getting sick and being unable to work. She was afraid of death and was even more terrified of having an incurable disease that she would have to live with and suffer through for many years. Her mind went on and on until she finally fell into a restless sleep.

The next morning, the blood bank called and said they just needed the dates of when she had gone to El Salvador for a medical mission the year before so that they could complete their paperwork. That's it. No diagnosis of AIDS. No cancer. They just wanted some routine information for their records. From that simple voicemail, her mind generated a deluge of thoughts that she tortured herself with all night. In hindsight, she realized that she should have just waited to hear from them before letting her thoughts get completely out control over absolutely nothing.

Whether we are faced with simple choices, imagined crises or a true life-changing event, the best thing to do is to make a decision and then go forward. When a dear friend of mine found out her breast cancer had returned and that she would need to go through a second surgery followed by chemotherapy and radiation, she was understandably shocked. There were so many reasons for her to be worried. As it had recurred within a year, the tumor was thought to be aggressive. Her two children were still so young. And of course, she would have to deal with the hair loss, fatigue, pain, nausea and all the other complications of treatment. But instead of dwelling on these things, she made up her mind to go forward and to fight the cancer with everything she had. She was able to laugh at herself while trying on funny-looking wigs that didn't fit her or looked completely fake. She took her kids out for little day trips whenever she felt well. With each chemo treatment, she would send out defiant text messages like, "Bring it on," in response to her friends' concerns and well wishes. She did it without asking, "Why me?" She understood that the physical aspect of dealing with recurrent breast cancer was difficult enough that she didn't need to "mark up" her journey with self-pity and anger. She did what she had to do and just kept on going. As the poet Robert Frost said, "The best way out is always through."[4]

We experience life through what we perceive with our five senses as well as the thoughts that already exist in the background of our minds. Whenever something comes to our attention, the information we gather is then processed somewhere in our brains so that we can understand and react appropriately. At this most basic level of thought and reaction, the experience of life is like raw organic food. But when we add intellectual and emotional baggage, it's as if we dump a truckload of salt, preservatives and artificial flavorings into what had been so pure and natural. The result is an unhealthy and over-processed meal that makes us sick, especially if we continue adding on internal drama. But if we can receive and then digest information about the world around us with a minimum amount of navel-gazing and environmental conditioning, then life would be so much easier and more peaceful.

Everything in life, including our thoughts, has a price in terms of how much time and energy we spend on it. Some things, like deciding whether or not we want to go to the gym, in theory should be a no-brainer that requires very little of our energy, while more serious issues like cancer are much more expensive. In the end, though, we always have a choice in deciding how much we ultimately want to pay. And just like a ripe mango at the street market that's going for the fair price of 10 baht (about 30 cents), we should learn how to pay the price that something is worth and not a penny more.

True Beauty

While flipping through an airline magazine during a recent trip overseas, I came upon a travel article about Milan. In the article, the writer talked about how, with its posh nightclubs and restaurants filled with glamorous jet-setters, even the normal, nonfamous people looked as if they just had stepped out of a glossy magazine. Indeed, one of the photos that was part of the article showed two women walking out of a trendy boutique bearing shopping bags of haute couture. With their svelte figures and perfectly chiseled cheekbones, they could easily have passed as supermodels. Everything about the city seemed to represent the world's idea of beauty, as fleeting and ethereal as that may be.

And yet, when I thumbed just a few pages past the article, there was a photo of a young man in a T-shirt and shorts with longish hair tucked behind his ears. He was standing in an open-sided wooden shack surrounded by children somewhere in Africa. They were laughing and smiling as he shined a flashlight into the eyes of a little boy sitting on a makeshift examination table. The photo was from an advertisement for a volunteer physicians' organization that provided free medical care to the world's most underserved areas.

It was just a picture but it took my breath away, for it captured the very best of humanity. It was a portrait of an individual who cared so much for his fellow man that he would travel halfway around the world bringing with him all of his knowledge and training to help those who needed it the most. It was a striking contrast from the glistening streets of Milan. But the message that emanated from this photo of an individual giving of himself to better the human race was of true beauty, one that will last until the end of time.

The Big Picture

ometimes, we can't see the forest for all the trees. And sometimes, we just don't have the capacity to do so. In his book *Man's Search for Meaning*, the late author Viktor Frankl, a holocaust survivor and physician, writes that there is meaning in suffering even if we can't see it.[5] He illustrates his point with the story of an ape that was being used in research studies in the 1950s to test out polio vaccinations. The ape was repeatedly injected several times a day with various medications all for the sake of mankind. Unfortunately, the ape did not understand nor was it capable of understanding why it was constantly being jabbed by needles all day. Thus, to the ape all the pain and suffering caused by the injections was random and meaningless.

How many times have we found ourselves in a painful situation where we were emotionally or physically hurt and we asked that universal question: why me? What have I done to deserve this? Why am I in so much pain? What Frankl suggests with the example of the ape is that if we had the ability to look at the situation from another vantage point, there is indeed a reason for our suffering, that somewhere on a higher plane it does make sense. That it's not random and empty. That there really is a pattern, a divine order that we as mere mortals are not privy to. It's all there, but we can't see it because it lies beyond the limits of our understanding. It's like trying to picture a six-dimensional object. We just can't. We don't have the faculties to do so. And when we're suffering, it's difficult to be ultra-insightful, especially when we're in the middle of something that hurts so much we can't even see straight.

Frankl's analogy is at once profound and illuminating. It can be helpful in our daily lives to consider the idea that there *is* meaning in our suffering, even if it never comes to light. Suffering in itself is a result of wanting life to be a certain way and not being able to accept it when things turn out differently. It doesn't matter what it is that we hope for: green traffic lights on our way to work when we're running late, a lab test to come out negative for a bad disease or a quick end to a painful divorce. It's all the same on different scales. We just want things to turn out the way we want them to. And when they don't, we become irritated, angry, sad, frustrated or deeply depressed. We often take things personally, when in reality sometimes things just are the way they are.

There are so many forces at work in the universe that are completely beyond our scope of understanding. If we can at least accept this, then we don't have to get upset when we are stopped at a red light. We can face our medical illness with dignity and courage. And we may even find the strength to go another round with the divorce lawyers. The point is that we just have to keep going and remind ourselves that everything happens for a reason. We must have courage and move forward, taking it one day at a time. As my friend once said, if anything else, suffering creates places in our hearts that we never knew existed.*

*He was paraphrasing the 19th century French writer, Leon Bloy, who wrote, "Man has places in his heart which do not yet exist, and into them enters suffering in order that they may have existence."

Sifu's Wild Ride

I love garbage day. With the week's trash gone from my home, I feel cleaner and lighter. But mostly, I'm relieved to dispose of any raw meat products like the fatty trim off a chicken breast, the skin from a piece of raw salmon or any other potential source of harmful bacteria. One wintry Cleveland morning, I woke to find my mother (who I now call Sifu, which is Chinese for "teacher") in her saffron pajamas hurriedly cutting up chicken in the kitchen. Although she is now a Buddhist monk living in a rainforest temple in Thailand, my mother still insists on cooking for me when she comes to visit. The rush on the chicken that morning was because it was garbage day, and she was trying to finish up so that she could bring the unwanted chicken parts and packaging out to the curb before the garbage men came. I tried reassuring her that she had plenty of time, but she was still chopping away on the cutting board when I left for work that morning.

An hour later, I was in the middle of seeing a patient in clinic when one of the other physicians interrupted us to let me know someone needed to speak to me. I apologized to the patient and stepped out of the room. There in the middle of the hallway was Sifu, who was still wearing her saffron pajamas and a pair of slippers. While she stood there calmly with a serene expression on her face, I was wide-eyed and flustered. The conversation went something like this:

"Sifu, are you okay?"

"Everything's fine. I just need the keys."

"What happened? How did you get here?"

"I locked myself out, but I'm okay. I came here in the garbage truck. I just need the keys. Sorry to bother you at work."

"A garbage truck? What? Just wait a minute and I'll take you home."

"Oh no, my friends are waiting for me downstairs. I just need the keys."

"What friends?"

"Hurry, they can't park there that long. I just need the keys, please."

Still in shock, I mechanically reached in my pocket and gave her the house keys. She said thank you and within seconds she disappeared from the hallway, leaving me completely and utterly confused. I went back to the room and finished seeing my patient. At the first opportunity, I called my mother to find out what had happened.

Apparently, the garbage truck had come unusually early that morning, and my mother found herself running outside in her pajamas in 30-degree weather with trash in hand. As soon as she heard the door close behind her, she knew that she had locked herself out. When the garbage men pulled up in the driveway, she told them what happened and asked for help. They offered to call me, but she didn't know my cell phone number and could only think to tell them that I worked at the hospital a couple of miles away. The two garbage men looked at each other and then looked at my poor mother shivering in her pajamas at the edge of the driveway. They radioed their supervisor and after several minutes of calling back and forth, my mother climbed up into the cab of the truck (not the back part as I had originally thought) and went for her first ride in a giant garbage truck.

The front entrance to the Cleveland Clinic is a circle drive that surrounds a beautiful glass-encased fountain. Patients pull up in the drive and are often awed by the massive glass multistory building that curves around the fountain and towers over the campus. Similar to an airport drop-off area, cars are allowed to stop briefly in the drive to drop off patients, but are then rapidly guided toward the parking lot to make way for other cars. That day, there must have been some important dignitary or official visitor coming as there were several men in valet uniforms and a couple of people in business suits waiting in the circle. Little did they expect a huge garbage truck with a burly driver, a petite Asian woman sitting in the front and another sturdy looking fellow hanging on to the back pull up in the fancy driveway. One of the men in suits went up to the truck and opened the door. Before he could say anything to the driver or tell him to use the back entrance, my little mother, who is not quite five feet tall, bald as monks tend to be, and still in her saffron pajamas hopped down from the truck with a cheery hello and walked right into the Cleveland Clinic, past all the open-mouthed faces of the formal greeting party. They continued to stare as she disappeared into the lobby elevator.

I can only guess what they were thinking. With her bald head, she could easily be mistaken for a cancer patient going for chemotherapy treatment, especially as the neurology department is in the same direction as the cancer building. Perhaps they thought the driver was her husband who was a Vietnam War veteran and had brought her back from the war. Who knows? In the end, my mother got the keys from me, hopped back into the truck, which was still parked out in the circle drive, and was able to get into my house safe and sound.

This is Sifu. This is my mother. She couldn't care less about appearances, calmly finds solutions to problems and tends to bring out the best in people. The two men who brought my mother to the hospital took time out of their busy day and very labor-intensive job to help another human being in need. This story is also about them and their act of selflessness. Giving someone a ride may not seem like a big deal, but it meant so much to my mother and especially to me. I will be forever grateful for their kindness and continue to wish them well every week when I bring my garbage out to the curb.

I used to love garbage day. But now I love my garbage men.

Better Than Ibuprofen

M any years ago, a young man walked into my office and told me that he had been experiencing frequent headaches for several months. When I asked him if he thought stress was a trigger, he told me "Yeah, my girlfriend said you might tell me it's stress-related." When I asked what he took for pain, he replied, "Sometimes, I take some of my wife's ibuprofen and it helps a lot." Confused, I asked, "Wife? I thought you said you had a girlfriend." Without missing a beat he said, "I have a wife *and* two girlfriends. They fight all the time." Aha.

I finished the neurologic examination and gave him a prescription for what appeared to be a tension headache. I also recommended that he consider breaking it off with at least one woman in his love quadrangle as all the drama was likely contributing to his headaches. He thought about it for less than a minute and said his wife would be the one to go. Yes, definitely my wife, he concluded. I just shook my head and wished him well.

Sometimes, the source of our headaches is of our own creation. We can easily complicate our lives with a series of poor choices that are driven by what we think will make us happy contrary to what our brains tell us. It's amazing how when we really desire something, when we feel that we have to have it no matter what the cost, all logic and reason go out the window. Then we're stuck dealing with the repercussions of our actions and that thing that we wanted, that we thought was absolutely necessary for our happiness and well-being doesn't turn out to be so great after all. The good news though is that if we understand this and take steps to remedy the situation, correct our ways and try to be less selfish, we can fix the problem ourselves and the headache goes away. It's better than ibuprofen and much cheaper than a divorce.

A Mother's Day Card

I t's different when it's your kid. This is what all of my friends tell me when we hear the not-so-distant wail of a small child at a restaurant or, worse yet, the screams coming from the row behind us on a plane as we take off on a cross-country flight. When I asked my mother about this, she said that it is different. Your first thought is about the child's well-being. You worry if he or she is okay, but you also worry about the people around you. And of course, you want the child to be quiet if possible. I then asked my mother, "What do people actually think of when they see their child?" She said that most people look at their kids and think of them as an extension of themselves out there in the world.

"So am I like your arm or your leg?" I asked.

She looked at me and said, "You are my heart."

Happy Mother's Day, Sifu.

bloom

Take Yourself Out of the Equation

Although informal polls lack the rigorous analysis of scientific research, I've always found them to be rather entertaining and somewhat informative in that they provide a glimpse into what people are thinking. For instance, a recent nationwide survey revealed how Americans felt about Washington politics when it was found that root canals, traffic jams and head lice were all rated more favorably than Congress. But perhaps a more revealing poll done many years ago was one that tried to determine what people feared most. Cancer and loneliness made it to the top ten as expected, but the most commonly reported fear was public speaking.

I was surprised at first but on second thought, I realized that it's not that people would actually rather die than speak in public, although the comedian Jerry Seinfeld once said that some of us would prefer being in the casket to giving the eulogy at a funeral. It's just that most of us don't think of dying on a regular basis. It's far off in the future, something that happens to us when we're old and gray. In contrast, what we do think about and deal with every single day is ego death. In our minds, the possibility of being humiliated, insulted or belittled is more likely to happen at any moment than physical death. When our bodies die, even if it's a horrible death, we don't have to worry about the social fallout afterwards. But if our egos die, if we are publicly humiliated especially in front of our friends, families and coworkers, we have to live with the pain of that experience every day for the rest of our lives.

Everyone has his or her own personal catalogue of shame. Some experiences, like being a victim of abuse or severe bullying, are understandably serious and life-altering. Other things that may have happened to us in the past might not really seem that bad when we try to explain it to someone else or when we analyze it in our minds later on. But at the moment that it happened, we may not have had the wisdom and life experience to fully understand it. So we end up holding on to all those thoughts and emotions, storing them deep in our memories. And with any trigger that brings it up in our minds, we can feel sadness or shame all over again. It could be an instance in childhood when someone made fun of us or perhaps we made a fool of ourselves in front of other people.

Even something as commonplace as stumbling while walking can be embarrassing if we trip and fall in front of several people. While it may not result in an emotional scar that comes up repeatedly in our memory, it can certainly affect our self-esteem and behavior. While jogging on a treadmill at a trendy upscale gym, my friend got his tennis shoe caught on the motorized track. He lost his balance and fell rather ungracefully off the machine, hitting his head on the side of the handrail as he went down. Although he picked himself up immediately, the people next to him all saw what happened and asked if he was hurt. "Just my pride," he answered as he headed for the exit as fast as he could. He was so embarrassed he couldn't go back to the gym for at least a few weeks.

The late S.N. Goenka, a highly respected Burmese meditation teacher, describes the ego in terms of a little statue or porcelain image that we create in our minds to represent ourselves. When we do something foolish or someone says something mean to us, the image in our own mind breaks, causing us varying degrees of emotional pain and distress. What's worse is that we project copies of these images onto other people so that if someone witnesses or finds out about something that happened to us that may have diminished our ego or image, our projections are damaged as well — magnifying the problem several times over. For example, it's one thing if our spouse speaks to us sharply or says something unkind in a private conversation at home, but if he or she yells at us in front of all of our friends at a dinner party, not only does the image within our own mind shatter, but the multiple images that we've created and projected onto everyone at that party shatter as well, increasing the pain of humiliation exponentially.

The bigger and more perfect the image we create, the more protective we are of preserving what we think is being projected onto the world around us. Imagine having to carry this fragile porcelain image with us at all times, always afraid that it will chip, scratch or break. This leads to anxiety, defensiveness, self-doubt and fear. We are afraid to do something that will make people think less of us. We fear that someone will damage our image by criticizing us, treating us badly, or making us feel insignificant. We worry that we will not be able to keep up our appearances and become ever more self-conscious. Not only that, but we have to spend a lot of time and energy maintaining our image, reinforcing it externally with more money, more prestige and more people to love and admire us. Unfortunately, it becomes a bottomless need for "reinforcements," which only make the image even more fragile and unstable. It's a never-ending cycle.

Now imagine having no image, no ego, nothing to constantly protect and maintain. Suddenly, it doesn't matter what anyone says or thinks about us. We can interact with the people around us with ease. We can go about our day peacefully without being self-conscious or anxious. When the sense of self is gone, we are absolutely free. It's a similar feeling to what we can experience with deep meditation, when we run or when we are completely absorbed in an activity where the self just melts away and we become part of the natural flow of things around us. The fear of failure, fear of humiliation — all of it is gone. Without ego, we can do anything.

So how do we stop creating these little images that require constant vigilance and protection? How do we let go of all this fear and anxiety? We have to take ourselves out of the equation. In any situation, if we can check our fears, desires and agenda at the door, the suffering is gone. With no ego, no self, then who can suffer? If we step back and remember the last time we felt a little depressed, we'll recall that all of our thoughts at that moment were focused on ourselves, *our* feelings, *our* lives. It was all inward thinking in which we were completely self-centered. It follows then that the first thing we can do is to stop navel-gazing and start looking outwards. Recognize that we as individuals are not the only person in the universe. It can be as simple as just understanding that when we're stuck in traffic, other people are stuck, too. Looking at all the slow-moving cars around us, we'll see taxis with nervous passengers trying to make it to the airport on time, minivans full of kids trying to get home after soccer practice and businessmen on their way to a meeting across town. We all have places to go and things to do. And when it really comes down to it, the truth is that each person is just focused on his own little world so that no one is really keeping score of all of our successes and failures except us. The late David Foster Wallace captured it best when he wrote in his book *Infinite Jest*, "You will become way less concerned with what people think of you when you realize how seldom they do."[6]

Along those lines, we should try and think of others first. Every day we can look for ways to be kind and considerate. A friend of mine once told me that if you're feeling down about yourself, do something nice for someone else. Go out of your way to help another human being and it will instantly make you feel better. I have found this to be true time and time again. It doesn't matter how great or small the effort, a single act of kindness can have tremendous implications for both the giver and the recipient. This is because the act of giving fulfills us and builds our self-confidence in ways that shiny awards and public recognition can never do. Little by little, it replaces the ego and all of its demands with an inner strength and joy that cannot be broken or shattered.

One of my patients, a lovely woman in her 50s with a chronic neurologic disease, had come to the hospital for back-to-back appointments with various specialists. By the time she got to my office, she was several minutes late but apologized profusely. When I looked down at her pants, I saw that they were wet. She smiled weakly and said she'd had an accident. At first I thought she'd spilled something and almost joked that it looked like she had wet herself, but then she said that she was having bladder problems again. Even though she was probably uncomfortable and embarrassed, she tried to reassure me that she was okay and was ready to proceed with the appointment. I told her that it was not okay and went out to the hall to get one of the nurse aides to help us. The nurse aide immediately came into the room, took one look at the patient and then spent the next 10 minutes making phone calls and running all over the hospital. She came back with a fresh pair of scrub pants and then led the patient to the bathroom so she could change. When the patient returned, now dry and clean, she was so grateful she gave us both a hug — a real hug. That meant more to me than any gift, award or title that I could ever receive. And it showed me how much it can mean to someone when they are given back their dignity.

Another important point is that we cannot base our self-esteem on external feedback. This only leads to insecurity, increased fragility and a very unstable sense of self-worth that constantly goes from one extreme to another. It can lead to depression and even suicide in people with pre-existing mental health issues as we've seen from the heartbreaking stories of young people who become victims of toxic opinions that are targeted towards them and posted anonymously about them online on social networking sites. Our self-esteem should be based on what kind of person we are, our thoughts and actions, and how we interact with the world around us. It is a dynamic process that can always change for the better if we consciously try to do the right thing. If we can start to think well of others, become more giving and take care to be kinder with our words, we will feel better about ourselves regardless of what other people say or think about us.

If someone offers us advice or even constructive criticism that will help us be a better person, then we can decide how much we want to change and then incorporate these suggestions into our lifestyle. But there will always be someone who doesn't like us and may try to put us down out of spite, envy or whatever reason. If that individual's intentions are not well meaning, then we don't have to give him or her the time of day. We can just smile or nod, and then walk on. On the other hand, if we really work to be a good person and help others, there will be people who will recognize that and be supportive of us. This can give us even more strength and make us immune to all the negative comments that aren't particularly helpful or constructive.

We also have to learn to forgive. People can say and do cruel things especially when they are unhappy and unfulfilled. When we're young or don't fully understand the situation, we can take these comments to heart and let them shape our sense of who we think we are. This can even trigger the creation of the porcelain image. But in the end, we are the ones who continue to build upon it and carry it with us for the rest of our lives. If someone told us many years ago that we weren't good enough or smart enough and we still keep it in our heads, then we are the ones telling ourselves that now. That person is long gone. But even if they are still a part of our lives, unless they're constantly standing in front of us and actively repeating those negative words, when we think of it and hear it in our heads, it's still our voice telling us this not theirs. So we have to go back to the source and understand that anyone who intentionally hurts another human being cannot be in his right mind and is likely a sick individual with many deep-seated issues. Thus, there is absolutely no reason to allow those words to have any further bearing on our lives. Whatever he or she said is now in the past and that's were we have to leave it. Forgive them and let it go.

And of course, we have to forgive ourselves. Sometimes, we can be our own worst critics. All of us have made mistakes in our lives. It doesn't help to keep beating ourselves over the head about something that already happened, even if we're still living with the consequences of our choices. Everything in life is a lesson and if we just use our mistakes as opportunities to learn, then we can and will be better. We are not perfect, but we can get up and keep going, keep fighting until we reach a place where we can accept who we are and know that we have done our best.

This is how we take ourselves out of the equation. The result is peace and a true sense of happiness. And according to multiple surveys of thousands of people, that's what we all want most in this world.

The Anatomy of Pain

There was nothing wrong with her eyes. Pale blue, they reacted well to the light that I shined into them shortly after she was brought to the hospital with an acute stroke. Yet, the 62-year-old woman who lay before me in the intensive care unit was now completely blind. The stroke had damaged the part of her brain that processed vision so that her blue eyes saw nothing. But there was another problem. She had absolutely no idea that she was blind. The interpretative area of the brain that would have allowed her to recognize a defect in her vision had also been affected by the stroke. So when I asked her if she could see the two fingers I held up in front of her face, she said the room was too dark. When I informed her that the light was on and that I wanted her to count my fingers, she told me to stop moving them around. For every question or command that had to do with her vision, she would come up with an excuse for why she couldn't see. She soon became frustrated with the examination so I finished up quickly and let her rest for the night. Although she ended up doing fine while in the hospital, during her time there she never recovered her sight nor did she ever realize that she was blind.

The anatomy of the brain is fascinating in that its organization and all of its connections affect how we experience the world around us. While jogging through my neighborhood one morning, I smelled fabric softener coming from a nearby apartment building. It immediately took me back to my childhood when I would help my mother fold the laundry fresh out of the dryer, the strong scent of fabric softener still clinging to our clothes. It's well known that smells can often trigger a memory more powerfully than the sense of touch, sound or even sight, because the part of the brain that processes smell is so close to the area that controls memory.

Similarly, there may be an anatomical reason for why the memory of physical pain is so short-lived once the pain is gone, but the memory of emotional pain can last a lifetime. We can find examples of this in our own lives. If we think back to a time when we were in the midst of severe physical pain, many of us would say and do almost anything to make it go away. And the longer it goes on, the more desperate we become. But once it's gone, when we are completely pain free, sometimes it's like it never even happened. The visceral nature of the pain is no longer there and even when we try to remember it, we don't actually feel the pain. We just remember what we thought and felt at that time that it was happening.

For women, it would be like the memory of childbirth, which is universally considered one of the most painful human experiences and is often used as a standard measure of severe pain. When people say something was "worse than childbirth," we know it was bad even though the subjective quantification of pain is so widely variable. Yet, many women often "forget" the discomfort of trying to sleep at night in their third trimester, the persistent backaches, the sickening nausea and of course the extreme pain they felt when their pelvic bones spread apart and their most fragile tissues were torn to shreds. Some forget everything as soon as the baby is born and are more than willing to go through it all over again when they opt to have more children.

But when something happens to us that's emotionally devastating be it abuse or a painful divorce, it is not easily forgotten. This is also true for things in our lives that might not be as traumatic but still made us feel small or humiliated all the same like being teased as a child, ridiculed in public or the last one picked for a team. Emotional pain often involves other people and is very complex. It comes in various combinations of anger, sadness, fear, anxiety and even thoughts of vengeance. It also cuts deeper than physical pain and can create scars that last for a lifetime. But the unique feature of emotional pain that distinguishes it from all other forms of pain is that it can still hurt months, years, even decades later. It can grab hold of us at any time and provoke the same feelings of rejection, humiliation and everything else we had felt previously, if not more so, in the moment that it comes back into the conscious mind. Most people keep these memories buried deep inside where they accumulate and then come up over and over again only to have more thoughts, more drama added to them. Over time, all of these memories and their associated intellectual and emotional baggage create holes in the heart that become the root of our fear and unhappiness.

We all have these holes although many of us don't see them. We dig them ourselves in an attempt to bury our memories and all the pain that went along with it. Then we blindly try to fill the holes with entertainment, alcohol, drugs, sex, material possessions, even work — any kind of distraction that keeps us from having to deal with what truly ails us. The truth is that many people are afraid to be alone with their thoughts. They subconsciously fear and avoid the restlessness, boredom and other unpleasantries they may encounter in their minds when everything is silent, when everything is turned off. We just have to look around us at the airport, the mall or even on the streets. People constantly have to be engaged in some form of activity. They're on their cell phones, surfing the web, emailing, texting, or tweeting. Some people still carry magazines or newspapers with them wherever they go so that if there's a lull in their lives like when they're waiting in line for something, they can just whip it out to fill the time. At home or in the car, people have the radio or television on for background noise to drown out all of the thoughts in their heads. Yet, none of these things really help and they often just make the situation worse by habituating people to being perpetually stimulated, which is fast becoming the baseline state of existence in modern society.

To definitively heal emotional pain, we have to stop relying on all of these external distractions, which are really just Band-Aids and not very good ones at that. We must fix the underlying problem and fill the holes. Fortunately, there are a number of ways to do this. For those of us who are not already spiritually transcendent beings or made of emotional Teflon, we can embark upon a path in which we learn how to give, have kindness, be grateful and accept things as they are. But the most important step, the one that trumps all others is the practice of mindfulness. This is how we can stop the constant internal dialogue, the endless cycle of thoughts that adds emotional and intellectual baggage to all of our memories and becomes the source of our emotional pain.

To practice mindfulness is to be consciously aware of our thoughts without judgment, watching them objectively as they come into our minds and then letting them go without holding on to them. This gets us out of our heads so that we can catch ourselves before getting caught up in a chain of thoughts that brings with it a whole host of emotions that can change our mood in an instant. It can ruin our day or in some cases trigger feelings of depression that can last for much longer.

The chain of thoughts can start with something so trivial as turning on the radio in our car and hearing a song that makes us remember someone we dated many years ago. Initially, it may be a sweet memory of when we first fell in love, but then we start to remember the little things that bothered us like the way the other person chewed his food or a stinging comment he said to us at the beach that summer. Then we remember the arguments, the accusations and all the anger and hurt we felt when it was finally over. Within a few moments, we go from the neutral feeling of turning on the radio to the warm memory of a past love, to the anger and bitterness of a bad breakup. If we don't pull ourselves out of that chain of thoughts we can keep remembering the terrible things that were said, other relationships that had not ended well, and so on.

Each chain of thoughts, even if it seems harmless at first, builds on itself and contributes to our mental framework that defines who we are and how we respond to things in our lives. With time, it evolves into a complex pattern of thoughts that we store somewhere in our minds so that it becomes a part of our stream of consciousness, influencing all of our daily experiences. We can come to a situation with fear, regret, anxiety and all sorts of emotional baggage based on these thought patterns. When we have positive thoughts, we feel good about ourselves and for a moment all is right in the world. But as soon as the positive thoughts fade away, they can then be replaced by negative thoughts or a bad memory, which in turn can darken our mood as what happened with the song on the radio. Back and forth, the mind wavers, bringing up emotions that affect how we act and feel on a moment-to-moment basis.

However, when we practice mindfulness we are actively watching our thoughts so that when a painful memory is triggered, we immediately see it for what it is. It's just a repetitive pattern of thoughts, something that is not an intrinsic part of us and can be actively discarded without further ado. The key is to catch the thought as soon as it comes up, recognize it as something separate from us like a visitor who's just passing through and then let it go before the entire drama of the memory plays itself out again. If we can break the chain of thoughts right then and there so that there is no ensuing emotional baggage, then that memory — that pattern of thoughts we've kept inside for so long — cannot hurt us. It really is just a thought, like the recognition of feeling cold on a winter day. It's a response to our external surroundings. Likewise, in the example of the song on the radio that brought back the memory of a soured relationship, we can objectively see the thought of a past love as just a response to the song we heard and nothing more. Even if the memory seems to arise spontaneously in our minds with no external trigger, we can think of it as a response to some unknown stimulus that came from within the mind. At the end of the day, a thought is just a response to some internal or external stimulus and in itself does not define us.

With time and continued practice, mindfulness leads to understanding, wisdom and then acceptance. These steps are critical and the means by which we can truly let go of emotional pain. Again, a painful memory is just a repetitive pattern of thoughts. Sometimes, the pattern just needs to be shifted or changed so that it can no longer affect us. Like a bacteria that can be genetically engineered to become a life-saving medicine, a painful memory from our past can be changed with understanding, which allows for complete resolution and then letting go. Just a small insight can make all the difference in the world. Even if the insight happens to come from other people, the practice of mindfulness allows us to be open to their ideas and suggestions so that we can assimilate them into our own thought processes, leading us to the same final pathway of understanding and then acceptance.

A friend and former colleague of mine is an extremely compassionate and sensitive physician who spends an immense amount of time talking with his patients and getting to know them so that he can provide the best care possible. Early in his career he developed an affinity for one particular patient who was his mother's age, a sweet and gentle woman who had multiple sclerosis, a brain disease that requires close monitoring. Over the years, she and her husband grew very fond of him and treated him as if he were their son, bringing him baked goods and other little gifts whenever they came for their appointments. She told all her friends about him and referred many other people to see him, even if it was for a disease out of his specialty just because she thought he was the best doctor she'd ever had. Towards the end of her life she started to have some mild burning pains in her feet. He prescribed her a very benign and safe pain medication that is also used for children with seizures. Although it did help alleviate her symptoms, she eventually passed away from another unrelated illness.

bloom

Shortly after her death, he received a nasty letter from the patient's son, who was also a physician. The letter was full of personal attacks on my friend, calling him unprofessional and uncaring and went as far as to blame him for the patient's death, citing the use of that pain medication as the reason. My friend was shocked, not just at how vicious and mean the letter was, but also that his patient had had a son. In the many years they had known each other, she had never mentioned him let alone the fact that he was a physician. Nevertheless, my friend kept the memory of that letter's terrible words in his heart for several years and every time it came up, he felt so ashamed, so sorry that he had not provided better care until he brought it up over lunch one day.

When he told me the story, I reassured him that he had provided outstanding care for that patient as he did with all of his patients. Then we figured out that there was probably a reason that this woman who had always been open and honest with him had never told him about her son. There was likely a falling out some time ago between the two of them, and the letter was written by the son out of anger, guilt and perhaps even a little jealousy toward my friend who had in some ways taken his place. With this new insight, he was able to change his pattern of thoughts from that of being criticized as a horrible physician lacking professionalism and compassion to the simple reality of receiving a letter from a grieving son who was grappling with many issues in the aftermath of his mother's death. With that small but permanent shift in his pattern of thoughts, he was able to let go of a memory that had hurt him for many years.

Only through the process of understanding can we really let things go. Unfortunately, no matter how much we want them to, all those people who hurt us, made us feel irrelevant or just plain bad about ourselves are not going to suddenly line up at our door to apologize and beg for our forgiveness. Nor does time really heal all wounds, especially the more serious ones that hurt us profoundly. More often than not, we have to be the ones who face up to our painful memories, understand what happened and then put it to rest once and for all. In the beginning, mindfulness will help us deal with the intrusion of these memories throughout our daily lives so that we don't have to keep filling the silence with distractions. Then with time and regular practice, it brings wisdom and opportunities to gain a deeper insight into our problems. Along the way we can get help from friends, family, books and even professional counseling if we need it. The end result is understanding and a shift in the pattern of thoughts that short-circuits the longstanding connection between memory and pain, allowing us to experience thoughts objectively without all the unnecessary drama, so that a thought is just a thought and nothing more.

Ultimately, the goal is not to repress the memory or try to get rid of it. It will always be there somewhere in the recesses of our minds. We just learn to let it be as it is. It's like the scar on my left elbow that I got from falling off the base of an outdoor sculpture when I was 7-years-old. It's a thick and wrinkled flesh-colored scar that marks where the concrete sidewalk had sliced open my elbow decades ago, but it doesn't hurt when I touch it. And even when I try to remember the pain I must have felt when I landed on my arm that day, I can only recall seeing the big gash on my elbow and blood oozing out of the fresh wound. I didn't cry over it then, and there's certainly no need to now as the pain is long gone. The scar is simply a reminder for me to be more careful. Sometimes, I even forget it's there.

bloom

The Bus Driver

ast week I met a woman who did not believe in the concept of vacation. She wasn't a corporate tyrant, nor was she a miserly spinster wary of any expensive frivolities. She drove a bus for developmentally disabled adults. Many of her passengers had severe autism, while others had brain damage due to birth defects or trauma, but all of them were mentally impaired. Each morning at 6am she would start picking them up one by one at their houses and take them to "work" at a special workshop where they made lids for soft drink bottles. She took care not to diverge from the regular route as some of the passengers would notice the change immediately and become agitated. They would start screaming and hitting themselves until the bus returned to its normal route and they could see the same houses and trees in the order they were accustomed to each morning.

Although most of them wore adult diapers, from time to time one of them would have an accident in his seat. She would calm him down by telling him that everything was okay and that he would be able to change as soon as they arrived at the workshop. For various reasons, she wasn't allowed to touch any of her passengers according to company policy, but she never really needed to anyway as they responded to her kind and reassuring voice. She finished the morning route by 8am and at 3pm she picked them up again at the workshop to take everyone home.

She told me that she had done this every day including Sundays and holidays for the last several years. When I asked her about vacation, she replied, "What about vacation? Why do I need vacation?"

"Well," I told her, "so you can rest."
"I can rest when I'm old."
"Don't you want to go to the beach?"
"And do what?"
"You could read and relax."
"I can do that at home. I love my job."

By any definition, it wasn't a glamorous job nor did it come with a lucrative salary. But it was enough to pay the bills. And most importantly, it was fulfilling. Every day she was able to do something good for another human being. She gave of herself to a group of people often forgotten by society, and she did it with her whole heart.

I told her there was a parking space in heaven reserved for her, and then I asked her to put in a good word for me. She laughed and promised that she'd do her best.

Something Sweet
for the Palate

One of my favorite restaurants when I lived in Virginia many years ago was a little burrito place near the water. The menu was simple: burritos, chips, salsa and these giant cookies that were almost as big as my face. One evening as a friend and I were at a table contemplating whether or not we had enough room for dessert, I watched a little girl who couldn't have been more than 4-years-old hesitantly make her way up to the counter toward the basket of cookies. That night the choices were oatmeal, peanut butter and chocolate chip, each clearly marked $1.00. The little girl's eyes grew wide as she peered over the side of the basket and took in the sight of all those cookies. In her hand were several dollar bills and some change, but she just stood there bewildered and unsure of what to say or do. The young man working behind the counter gave her a few moments and then gently asked her if she wanted a cookie. She nodded her head and extended her little hand with all the money in it, ready to give him everything she had. He smiled softly and took only a dollar, telling her to pick out any cookie she wanted. She reached for the chocolate chip cookie on top and smiled at the young man before she quickly turned around and ran back to her family.

I watched this from my table with great interest and was quite taken with the scene. I was touched by the young man's gentle manner, the little girl's innocence and the purity of their interaction. With his kind demeanor, he calmed her fears and took care of her needs without being annoyed or impatient. Nor did he take all of her money or more than the price of the cookie. Granted, I'm sure her parents were watching from their table as well, and there were many people in the restaurant that night. But for a moment it was just the two of them in that room. It was a meditation on loving kindness that I still remember fondly.

So many of us are missing that today. Everyone wants to be loved, to be cared for, to have someone be kind to us. It is often what we crave, what we need to make us feel whole, even if we don't know it. It's like when we've eaten an entire meal but still feel what we think is hunger. And so we eat more, snacking on chips, candy and other unhealthy fare just to make ourselves feel full. Yet, many times we're not really hungry. Nutritionists will tell us that when we don't feel full after eating a meal, sometimes it's actually because we're just thirsty. Instead of reaching for more food, we should instead drink a glass of water.

It's the same thing with loving kindness. Sometimes we feel like we're missing something from our lives. We think that maybe what we need is more clothes, a fancier car, a better job, a new partner or even plastic surgery to improve our appearance. We look all around us to find that missing piece when really what we need is kindness.

Kindness is not just an act of charity. It's the actual state of mind underlying it in which we genuinely care about another person's well-being. The amazing thing about it is that when we give kindness to others, it can be just as fulfilling as when we receive it ourselves. For example, we could ask a friend or coworker with a slight cough how he's feeling out of true concern for his health rather than just an empty social greeting. As he tells us about how he feels a little under the weather, we give him our full attention and then wish him a speedy recovery. On the receiving end, it's nice to know that someone cares about us even if it's just a brief encounter that ends with a get-well-soon wish. And on the giving end, when we ask the other person how he feels, we are putting aside our own agenda and stepping outside of our constant stream of thoughts (that often revolves around ourselves) to show another human being that we care for him. It's a small act of selflessness that we can cultivate into a habit, generating a new pattern of positive thoughts that over time can slowly change how we think, act and feel. It can bring us energy, self-confidence and even a sense of joy from within that cannot be found anywhere in the world around us. Material things may be able to fill us for a while, but the gift of loving kindness can fill us for a lifetime. And it can start with a single cookie.

bloom

Not Just Another Monday Morning Lecture

As a mandatory Monday morning lecture, "An Ethical Approach to Deep Brain Stimulation" doesn't even come close to sounding appealing. While the concept of brain stimulation itself is interesting in that a medical device implanted in the brain of a patient with Parkinson's disease can help him move better, this particular talk was focused more on the ethics of patient selection than on the surgery itself. Not only that, but it wouldn't include all the amazing before-and-after videos of patients who were severely disabled before the brain surgery and then afterward could miraculously walk or even play basketball again. I was so sure the lecture was going to be dry and completely irrelevant to my practice of neurology that I almost decided not to go. But I'm grateful that I did, because it turned out to be an insightful talk that nearly brought me to tears.

The speaker presented the cases from a humanistic standpoint, describing how patients felt when they were first offered surgery and then what happened after they regained the ability to move with the flick of an on switch. It was fascinating and often touching to learn how the surgery changed the patients' entire lives beyond the scope of just their disease. One case in particular actually fogged up my glasses.

It was the story of a patient who had recalled what he was thinking during the portion of his brain surgery when he was kept awake. This is a routine part of the deep brain stimulation procedure in which the operating team tells the patient to move certain parts of his body, activating mapped areas of the brain so that the surgeon would know which parts not to cut and where to safely put the stimulator. During a break in this part of the surgery, the patient suddenly had this feeling that he needed someone to hold his hand. He had a breathing tube down his throat and couldn't talk, so the only thing he could do was reach his hand out from under the surgical drape and move his fingers in the air. One of the nurses came over and intuitively took his hand, gently holding it in hers. As he recalled that moment in an interview after the surgery, he said "and for some reason I felt I needed that part and then it was okay. She had to go do something else and it was okay."

Fear, anxiety, worry — it could have been anything that drove that patient's need for a human touch. The man was in the middle of having his brain cut open so that a tiny machine could be placed inside his head. His whole life was about to change. He had a chance at getting better, but there was also a significant risk for permanent brain damage and even death. Yet, when that nurse took his hand, it meant the world to him. It reassured him that he wasn't alone, that everything was going to be okay. That small gesture was at once compassionate, tender and in its own way life-saving. The patient ended up doing very well and was grateful to the entire surgical team for his care. But out of that entire experience, it was the simple act of kindness when the nurse held his hand in hers that he will forever hold dear to his heart.

Payback

No good deed goes unpunished. This has become my friend's favorite saying whenever he goes out of his way to be helpful and then gets burned for it later. He's a very kind person and does a lot of volunteering and charity work in addition to being a full-time physician. Unfortunately, people sometimes take advantage of his good nature by unloading their work on him or burdening him with things that are markedly time-consuming and end up being above and beyond his normal duties. But he gives everyone a second chance and tries to think well of others even if their intentions are less than pure.

One evening when he returned home from work, he found that there was no electricity in the house. He and his wife were in the middle of a major renovation to their basement in which they'd updated the pipes, put in new flooring and even knocked down some walls to make space for a bathroom. That morning the contractor had been working on the electrical wiring, so naturally my friend called to let him know that he must have shut off the power somehow. The first thing the contractor said was that it wasn't his fault, that there was no way it could have been something he had done in the basement and that the problem must be coming from outside the house. My friend was tired after a long day at work and tried to hide the disbelief in his voice when he asked the contractor if he was sure because all the other houses in the neighborhood had power. The contractor, who had done a lot of work for them in the past and was actually a good guy, said he'd be right over to take a look at it although he remained firm that it wasn't his fault. It was already quite late that evening so my friend told him to just stay home with his family and that he could come by in the morning. He even joked that he and his kids would probably be able to survive one night without watching television or playing on the computer.

The next day, the contractor came over and worked for several hours trying to find the source of the problem. He even called an electrician friend of his to come over for free to help him figure out what was going on. They worked all day and finally they traced the problem outside to the power line coming from the utility pole down the street. The contractor had been right all along. When my friend called the electric company, they confirmed that it was indeed an issue with their wiring and sent someone out immediately. Within two hours, everything was fixed and they had power again. It was as if nothing had ever happened.

Most people would have blamed the contractor as soon as they saw that there was something wrong, and some may even have demanded that he come back to the house that evening to fix it. Even when my friend was first telling me about how the contractor had immediately said it wasn't his fault, I remember giving him an incredulous look and shaking my head as I was sure that the contractor was trying to pull a fast one on him. Because, really, what were the chances that an outside power line to a single house would go down at the same time that electrical work was being done within the home?

Sometimes kindness is just giving someone the benefit of the doubt even when it goes against all logic and common sense. Of course, if the contractor had had a pattern of sketchy behavior, then my friend would have handled things differently and probably would have fired him long ago. But that wasn't the case. The contractor had always been a good worker and had offered to come back to the house that night to check out the problem, despite being sure that it wasn't something he'd done. So even though my friend wasn't 100% certain about what had happened, he took the contractor at his word and trusted that they would sort things out the next day. The outcome was that when everything was fixed, there were no hard feelings. By erring on the side of the contractor, my friend was able to thank him for all of his hard work rather than having to apologize for not believing him and making him work extra for something that really wasn't his fault. He would also have been left feeling guilty and awkward about the whole situation, which could have affected the rest of the work on the basement. Instead, he was appreciative of the contractor's diligence, and the basement turned out great.

There was one other aspect about the whole incident that stood out in my friend's mind. It was the fact that the electric company had sent someone out right away and had everything fixed in less than two hours. He was actually more amazed by the utility company's promptness and efficiency than the entire issue with the contractor and the power line. He couldn't believe that everything had worked out so well and so quickly. "When have you ever seen that happen?" he asked me. I smiled and said it was payback from the universe for thinking kindly toward the contractor and letting him off the hook that night so that he could be with his family.

It usually doesn't happen right away or in the manner that we think it will, but a good deed eventually does come back full circle. I told him to think of it as a pat on the back from the universe. He considered it for a moment, knowing that it went against his rather pessimistic rule about good deeds being rewarded by not-so-good outcomes. Then he smiled in agreement and said he'd make an exception for this case.

Fair Is Fair

air is fair. That was my reasoning for tearing down my little
brother's brand new Star Wars poster when I was 6-years-old
and he 4. Although the only reason my mother had bought it
for him that morning was to keep him quiet while she was running
errands at the store, I took it as a gross injustice that there was no
Princess Leia poster for me. Insult was added to injury when my
brother teased me about how he was the only one with a poster and
proceeded to tape it up on the outside of his door. As soon as I saw
the giant picture of Luke Skywalker smiling down at me, I took it
upon myself to make sure that things were once again fair and tore
it down immediately. But the brief sense of satisfaction that came
with equalizing the situation quickly turned into remorse. To this
day, I can still remember the sharp crinkly sound of a large piece
of paper being torn in half and the long wail of pain and disbelief
that followed when my brother realized that his poster was no more.
Star Wars has never been the same for me since.

Although most of us eventually learn that life isn't always fair, it can still be upsetting when we experience injustice or when we hear about how other people were wronged in some way. For years, I simply could not understand the biblical story of the prodigal son and found it grossly unfair. In the story, the younger son of a wealthy landowner asks for his inheritance early and then leaves everyone behind to pursue a life of worldly pleasures. Meanwhile, his older brother stays at home, diligently toiling away on the farm and tending to the family. Years later, the younger brother returns home penniless, having squandered all of his money on women, gambling and other unsavory pursuits. When he goes to his father to seek forgiveness, not only does the father welcome him back with open arms, he then calls upon his servants to prepare a big feast in honor of the younger son's return. But not everyone shared his happiness. The older brother was angered at the ease by which the prodigal son was accepted back into the family, as well as the festivities that would be bestowed upon him after years of being selfish and self-centered. When he shared his dismay with his father and asked why had there never been a celebration for him even though he had worked so hard to look after the land and the family for all those years, his father explained that there was no need to throw him a party because he had been home the entire time. The end.

I couldn't believe that was the story's resolution. That was it? That was supposed to make everything better? On the contrary, I felt that it explained absolutely nothing and basically discounted all of the older son's loyalty and hard work. I understood that the part about the younger son was a metaphor for how we can always return to our spiritual home and be forgiven as long as we acknowledge our wrongdoings and strive to be better. But I didn't see the lesson to be learned concerning the older son until now.

The problem with the older son was that he expected something in return for all those years of staying at home and doing the right thing. His good acts were not pure nor were they truly selfless. There were strings attached. He was also self-righteous and looked upon his younger brother's behavior with condescension and disdain. It's possible that he may have even been a little jealous of him and resented the fact that his younger brother had been able to go out and enjoy himself while he had to stay behind as the "good son."

And therein lies the catch. If the older brother had really performed all of his duties as a good son out of the kindness of his heart, he too would have rejoiced in his brother's return to the right path. It's like celebrating someone's recovery after they've been sick for many years. If all along we've enjoyed good health because we've been eating nutritious food and exercising regularly, there's no reason for us to be angry or jealous when someone we know decides to follow suit after years of being a couch potato and gorging on fast food, even if that lifestyle was easier or more enjoyable. Sure, healthy food is not always as delicious as junk food. A chocolate bar tastes a lot better than a stalk of celery. And yes, sometimes we have to force ourselves to get up and exercise when we'd rather just take a nap. It takes effort to stay healthy, and it's not as fun or entertaining as doing things that are purely for pleasure. But it's the right thing to do for our bodies, and it's good for us in both the short and long term.

The older son could not see this, nor was he forgiving or generous in spirit. All he understood was that he had worked hard and received little if anything in return. Certainly, there's nothing wrong with wanting to be in good graces with our families or being recognized for our hard work, but it shouldn't be the main reason for why we do something as it renders the act of charity less than pure and takes away from the overall result. If our motivation for doing the right thing is at all related to the ego — even if it's just wanting some positive feedback, then we will often find ourselves disappointed because the feedback that we were waiting for is either not there or not as much as we think we deserved. Thus, we cannot reap the full benefits of our good acts.

The story of the prodigal son is not about what's fair and what's not fair. It's about doing the right thing for the right reasons, because that's what we're supposed to be doing anyway — even if there's nothing in it for us except for the sheer fact that we're following the right path. If we can continue on with the right motivation and the right intentions, then we will need nothing in return. The fulfillment will come from within. And that is a proper ending.

Turn Off Weather Please

On stepping outside one chilly winter morning, my 2-year-old nephew turned to his mother and said, "It's cold. Turn off weather please." Given his age, it's understandable that my little nephew thought that the world was a climate-controlled environment that could be adjusted to his comfort level with a giant thermostat in the sky. Unfortunately, we as adults often forget how so many things in life are beyond our control. It's common for many of us to become irritated or upset when we don't get what we want or there's a delay in completing our agenda because of traffic, inclement weather or any other factor that we can't change. It can be especially frustrating when our task depends on other people. Everyone has his or her own separate issues and reasons for doing things (or not doing things), which can disrupt even the most meticulous of plans. We ourselves can throw everything off course by trying out a new "shortcut" when driving somewhere or saying the wrong thing at the wrong time only to beat ourselves over the head about it later.

As most of us know first-hand, things often turn out in a way that's not what we had wanted or expected despite making well-founded predictions based on personal experience or established trends and patterns. For instance, to reduce our risk of cancer, we can choose not to smoke or try to avoid exposure to it altogether. Unfortunately, people who have never smoked a day in their lives are diagnosed with cancer every day. Likewise, exercise and nutrition are important for maintaining personal wellness, but every once in a while we'll hear about a health-conscious runner who dropped dead from a heart attack at the age of 50. The point is that anything can happen at any time.

In economics, a "black swan" is an event that occurs out of nowhere and changes the financial markets and everyday life as we know it forever. The terrorist attacks on 9/11 are a tragic example of a black swan with far-reaching consequences that are still being felt today. But we can have our own personal black swan in the form of a freak accident, the sudden loss of a job, or the unexpected death of a loved one. That one event can change our lives dramatically and yet there's not much we can do about it except to figure out how to handle the situation afterwards.

Certainly, it helps to be organized and to prepare for all sorts of potential outcomes, but in the end we have to acknowledge that there is only so much we can do and then let things be as they will. As the former heavyweight champion Mike Tyson once said, "Everyone has a plan until they get punched in the face." One of my patients, a very sweet 89-year-old woman originally from Brazil put it more eloquently when she gave me some parting advice at the end of our one and only appointment. This is what she said:

"What I've learned in my life is that everything we have is on loan. Nothing is really ours. The sun, the flowers, our bodies — nothing belongs to us. I first learned this when I was pregnant with my oldest child. He was so small, so tiny when he was born. For the first three days the doctors weren't sure if he would survive. Every day, every minute I didn't know if he was going to live or die. He did end up making it, but I realized then that it was all out of my control."

"I learned this again when my youngest son (here she paused and looked down for a moment) died at the age of 52 from thyroid cancer. In less than a year from when they told him he was sick, he was gone. He left behind a beautiful wife and baby son who will think of him every day for the rest of their lives as I do."

"We think we know things, but really we know nothing. Everything in life is about learning, but it's such a big lesson that we can never really learn it all."

There is much truth in her words, as sad and poignant as they were. We may not be able to learn it all, but if we pay close attention and really try to learn from our experiences, then we'll see that the only thing in life that we can really control is how we react to the world around us. With each lesson, our understanding will deepen and we can learn to accept whatever happens, come what may.

bloom

Don't Judge Me

E ven after several years of marriage, my friend's husband is still perplexed at how the clothes hangers keep disappearing from their closet. Whenever he can't find one to hang up his shirt with, he'll ask my friend where all the hangers went. She'll innocently shrug her shoulders and then try to look as bewildered as he feels. Later on, she'll go out and buy more hangers...and more clothes. Her trick is to keep her shopping bags in the trunk of the car and then bring them in with the groceries. Like many women, my friend loves to shop. And like many men, her husband is unable to understand why she needs more sweaters. Whenever he teases her about all the clothes she has, she'll reply with her favorite catchphrase, "Don't judge me." Although she always says it jokingly, it's a great line that serves as a nice reminder to think twice before passing judgment on another person.

When we judge people, we bring them into our frame of reference and measure them in terms of our own personal standards.

Unfortunately, we often do this based solely on their appearance, which is unfair and can result in an unfavorable impression that's also dead wrong. A few years ago, a friend and I were on our way to see a movie one evening and found a parking space right behind the theater. The problem was that it was metered parking and neither of us had any change. As we fumbled through the glove compartment and cup holders of the car, a beat-up brown station wagon pulled up right next to us. We looked up for a second and saw two young college-aged kids get out of the car dressed in clothing that could easily have been from a thrift store. They looked like they barely had enough money for themselves let alone any spare change for us. However, when they saw us tearing apart the car for quarters, not only did they put change in their meter but they put money in ours as well.

One of them, a young woman wearing a tattered coat and old wool hat, walked over to me and without saying a word handed me even more quarters for later. Stunned, I was at once grateful for their kindness and deeply ashamed that I had been dismissive of their ability to help me. I thanked them both profusely, but they just smiled and walked away. To the passerby, putting change in someone else's meter may seem like a small gesture, but to me it meant something so much more. In contrast to how quick I was to judge them, they simply saw us as two people who needed help and gave us what they could. They were an example of how we should strive to be everyday — selfless and kind.

Another issue is that we can never really know what's in another person's mind or the experiences that have shaped his life. And yet when we judge people, we assume that we do. When Hurricane Katrina devastated New Orleans in 2005 with violent storms and massive flooding, the people there who had not heeded the government's warnings to leave their homes ended up stranded on their rooftops or worse. In a call to the nation for help, a young Senator Obama stood on the Senate floor and reminded his fellow Americans that not everyone could throw some bottled water into the back of their SUV, drive to higher ground and then use a credit card to check into a hotel. While it sounds rather obvious, that's exactly what many people across the country, including myself, thought to some degree. I could not understand why the able-bodied people there did not just get up and leave when they were told about the storm. Only later did I realize that many of them lacked money (some didn't even have a bank account) and the resources to do just that.

Everyone is coming from different places. Death, divorce, poverty, abuse, illness, neglect — so many things can happen to a person that forever changes his life and how he reacts to things. Even people from the same family who grew up in the same household can have completely different experiences that affect the choices they make, right or wrong. If we can acknowledge and try to understand that, then we can have empathy and compassion for those who are suffering regardless of who they are or what path they took in life. It also helps to give us a better sense of appreciation and gratefulness for what we have.

In everyday life, we are constantly assessing the people around us. Part of it is necessary for functioning in society as we need to gather information about our environment to ensure our safety and complete our daily tasks. Most of our assessments are just an objective description of what we see — a little boy walking his dog, a coworker carrying a cup of coffee, a woman driving a car — and that's that. If we keep it at that level, then there's no drama and the story ends right there. The problem arises when we let our thoughts go a little farther and we start to judge. It may seem harmless if we're internally commenting on someone's outfit or lifestyle choice without voicing our opinion aloud, but it affects us in ways that we may not be aware of on a conscious level. This is because when we pass judgment on others, we bring our own ego and emotional baggage to the table, which leads to a chain of thoughts that can eventually influence our mood or state of mind. And because most of those internal comments tend to be critical and not very generous in spirit, they often result in feelings of irritation, displeasure and even anger at the other person, even if they didn't do anything to us.

For instance, if we see a woman on the street wearing revealing clothing, an objective assessment would be limited to the observation that the woman is wearing revealing clothing. When we judge her, however, the story goes on. We create a chain of thoughts, which begins with the internal comment that this woman is inappropriately dressed. We go on to think that she has poor taste and perhaps questionable moral character. This may then cause feelings of dissatisfaction with her appearance, followed by indignation, self-righteousness, moral superiority or a combination thereof. The result is that we've made ourselves unhappy just by thinking about how another person is dressed. But if we don't judge her and just see her as a human being doing the best she can to survive like the rest of us, then we can let her be and let our thoughts be. Any issues that arise out of this situation are purely of our own creation, as her existence and choice of dress are not for us to approve or disapprove.

On the other hand, when we refrain from judgment, we accept people just as they are. Life is hard enough. In this day and age, when everything from restaurants to health care is being publicly critiqued online and personal attacks are all over the internet, it's a welcome change when people can just leave each other be as long as they're not harming others. Many people have suffered greatly in their lives. Even if we had a similar experience, we can never truly understand what it was like for another person to go through what she did, what she endured and how she survived the aftermath of her trauma. For some, the scars are still there and can manifest in various ways including anger issues, defensiveness, unexplained fear, poor self-esteem and chronic pain. Instead of adding to these people's suffering by being judgmental of them because they don't seem to fit into what we think is "normal," we should instead offer them kindness or at least withhold our criticism and just let them be.

Not long ago, a woman in her 50s with perfectly coiffed hair and immaculate makeup came to see me in clinic for whole body pain. While she did have arthritis, the severity and widespread nature of her pain were markedly out of proportion to the minimal joint disease that she had. She had gone from one physician to another without any relief of her symptoms until she was referred to me to see if there was a nerve problem causing her pain. As I was typing away at the computer during our visit, she asked me about anxiety. "I have a lot of anxiety and I was just wondering, could stress be doing all of this? Could stress have been the cause of my arthritis? When I was a child, my brother did something to me. He — "

Tears began to well up in her eyes and she struggled to come up with the right words to express her deep-seated shame. In that moment I saw her sadness, the depth of her humiliation and so I stopped typing and finished her sentence. "He did something bad to you. Right?" She looked down at the floor, "Yeah, he did something bad to me." I gently told her that he didn't cause the arthritis. The stress didn't cause it either. She was probably genetically predisposed to having the disease, although any physical or emotional stressors could certainly worsen it. Whatever terrible thing her brother did to her so long ago had not led to the joint disease. She would have had it anyway.

I then told her she looked great. That she looked much younger than her age and that when I first came in the room I thought I had the wrong patient. Her face brightened and she smiled, saying that everyone told her that. Her husband chimed in and said she had a soap opera disease in that she always looked good despite having a terrible illness, like the actresses on TV who are supposed to be in a coma. They lie there in a hospital bed with oxygen tubing in their nose and yet their hair and makeup are perfect. I nodded my head in understanding, then pretended to be one of those soap opera actresses as I tossed my hair back, batted my eyelashes and said rather dramatically, "I'm dying." They both laughed at that. We then addressed her pain issues and she ended up doing very well with the appropriate medications.

Our job in this life is not to judge. It's to care. To help others. And if we can't help them, then we just learn to accept people as they are. When we can do this, it not only brings us peace of mind, but it generates an air of calm and comfort around us that makes it easy for others to be with us. Life is better this way for everyone, including those who have no spare hangers in their closet.

Just Make It to that Tree

A good friend of mine is one of those ultra-marathoners who runs 50-kilometer races...with hills...in cold and rainy weather...for fun. As I consider 30-miles to be a long way to *drive*, I asked him what kind of Jedi mind tricks he uses on those grueling runs to keep himself from getting tired, hungry or just plain bored. He told me that after about 10 miles, he'll get a runner's high where he feels like he could run forever. But then at 20 miles, his joints start to ache, everything hurts, he's cold, he's exhausted and his body is screaming for him to quit. When his mind starts questioning rather loudly why he's doing this, that's when he knows the race has just begun. Because that's when he has to fight his thoughts, his fears, his complaining mind. At that point, he no longer thinks about finishing the race and tells himself he's just going to make it to that tree up ahead. When he gets to the tree, he decides he just needs to make it to that large rock, then that sign and then that turn in the road. Little by little, he keeps going until he makes it all the way to the finish line.

The main issue is that he knows that the pain and exhaustion will go away shortly after he quits. But the actual quitting, the knowledge that he didn't finish what he started — that defeat lasts forever. So for him, long-distance running is an exercise in fighting his mind and winning.

Although most of us don't run 30-mile races, we all know what it's like to face what seems like an impossible task and ask ourselves, "How in the world am I going to do this?" The task can be something as simple as cleaning out a garage or coming back to a massive pile of work after being on vacation for a couple of weeks. But it can also be a more serious undertaking like going through a series of chemotherapy for cancer or trying to take care of an ill parent, kids and a busy household all at the same time. We can't start off by thinking about the enormity of the problem and how we're going to have to use superhuman strength to tackle it. Otherwise we'll just get frustrated and end up wasting time thinking about all the things we have to do without actually doing anything.

The trick is to forget about the finish line and set smaller goals within the context of the overall task, little milestones along the way that make things more doable. It's a matter of shrinking down our frame of reference so that we can get our heads around what we have to do. For example, if we're trying to lose 20 pounds and our weight seems to have leveled off several pounds short of our goal, we can stop thinking about the all the weight we have left to lose and just concentrate on getting to the gym at least three days a week for the next month. After that, we can increase it to four days a week or cut out sweets, changing things up month after month until we get to where we need to be.

Another example is when we have an out-of-control to-do list with things that absolutely need to be done. In those situations, we can remember what my mother always says, "You have two hands, one head and only 24 hours in a day. Do the best you can." The best way to start is to do one thing at a time. It doesn't even have to be the most important thing. For those of us with a never-ending inbox at work, I once attended a seminar for women professionals where the speakers recommended that we start with the most recent email and work backwards. It seems counterintuitive as the older emails have been sitting in the inbox for a longer period of time, but because the latest email likely pertains to something of more recent memory it's probably easier to take care of. Once we finish that, we can continue working backward until we get ourselves back into a comfortable rhythm that allows us to prioritize the messages however we wish as long as we keep things moving.

It's natural to sometimes feel overwhelmed by the length of the journey, but we can do it. We can do anything if we temporarily let go of the master plan and tell ourselves we're just going to make it to that tree. Step by step, we just keep going until we finally cross the finish line even if there are hills...cold and rainy weather...and it's no longer fun.

bloom

True Love

F airy tales are not what they used to be. In the classic Disney stories, a charming prince and beautiful princess fall madly in love with each other after only a brief song-filled encounter that often involves talking animals. But in today's revamped fairytales, the concept of true love is given a much-needed makeover. In the film *Maleficent*, a retelling of Sleeping Beauty, true love is now depicted more realistically in the form of a mother-daughter relationship between a princess and what turns out to be a very misunderstood fairy godmother.[7]

Although Maleficent originally curses the infant princess to fall into a coma on her 16th birthday as revenge for the king's betrayal of her love and trust, she is actually a kind fairy who secretly helped raise Sleeping Beauty along with her three fairy godmothers. As the fairy tale goes, the princess pricks her finger on a spindle and falls into a deep sleep that she can only awaken from with true love's kiss. To the surprise of many moviegoers, a kiss on Sleeping Beauty's lips from the hapless young prince she'd briefly met earlier on in the film did absolutely nothing. Only when Maleficent expressed her profound sorrow at what she had done to the princess in blind vengeance so many years ago and then bent down to kiss her on the forehead did Sleeping Beauty's eyes flutter open. As evident by the power of the second kiss, true love was not the infatuation between two young people who happened to cross paths in the forest for just a few minutes. It was the deep emotional bond that had formed over many years between a mother figure and her child, a bond that could never be broken even after one of them had fallen into a "death-like sleep."

True love is real. But it's usually not this intense passion that takes over our very existence so that nothing else in the world matters except for being with the one we love. Nor is it an endorphin-filled high in which the mere thought of the other person sends us floating up into the clouds. These are actually descriptions of infatuation, which we all know doesn't last. Instead, true love is a portrait of selflessness. It's about giving, understanding and kindness. It's doing what is best for the other person even if it means letting them go as heartbreaking as it may be.

True love makes us want to be a better person and to be what the other person needs. It's about their happiness not ours. With infatuation, the feelings that we have about the other person are all in reference to ourselves. It's about where we fit into the picture. We may genuinely want to do good things for the other person and wish them a wonderful life, but we're only happy if we get to be with them. And that's the difference. Infatuation is a self-centered form of love that is a reflection of *our* feelings, *our* dreams and *our* desires. In contrast, true love is not about us at all. It's about the other person's feelings, dreams and desires. When we truly love someone, we would willingly die for that person. But when we love with selfishness, we would kill anyone who threatens our relationship.

The 19th century writer Anthony Trollope once said, "There is no happiness in love, except at the end of an English novel." While this may be somewhat of an exaggeration, real life stories of true love are typically not as passionate or witty as what's depicted in romance novels. Yet, because real life stories actually happened, they're more tangible and can better capture the essence of selfless love than any work of fiction.

Several years ago, I saw a 60-year-old woman in the hospital who had a large mass creeping along the base of her skull that everyone suspected was an aggressive brain tumor. Unfortunately, the diagnosis couldn't be confirmed as the biopsy of her brain had to be stopped prematurely due to severe bleeding during the surgery. The patient was sent home on high-dose steroids with a plan to repeat her brain MRI and then follow up with me as an outpatient in hopes that the biopsy could be tried again in another spot.

A few weeks later her husband brought her back to see me in clinic for a check-up. Her face was swollen from the steroids and she spoke with a child-like voice that was the result of brain damage and severe confusion. She didn't remember me and couldn't tell me where she was or why she was there to see me. This woman who had raised four children, volunteered regularly at her church and was constantly baking cookies for her friends and family now needed assistance with even the most basic daily activities. Her husband had to help her with all of her meals, going to the bathroom and even walking into my office that afternoon. But I could see that he had been taking good care of her. She was wearing clean clothes and even had on a little lipstick. He had helped her with that, too, because she'd told him years ago that she always felt better when she was wearing lipstick.

After he carefully sat her down in the chair, I asked him to step into the hallway with me just outside the door so I could show him the latest MRI of her brain. It looked much worse than it did in the hospital. Although he'd been a factory worker most of his life with no formal education in medicine, he could see for himself that the brain mass had rapidly grown in the last few weeks. When I saw him take in a deep breath and hold it, I asked him if he was okay. Was he tired? Was it difficult having to watch her around-the-clock because she was so confused? He slowly exhaled. Then he looked at me, his eyes worn, his breath heavy with the smell of cigarettes and said:

"Yes. I am tired. I'm tired of having to go to all these doctors and make sure that everything's being covered by the insurance company. I'm tired of having to drive several hours to get here for all of her appointments. I'm tired of trying to find parking downtown and then walking all over your hospital. But am I tired of taking care of her? Never. I've loved her for 32 years. And I'll never get tired of her. Never."

I knew he meant every word. It was in the way that he held her when they walked into the exam room, how he was always at her bedside in the hospital trying to remember everything the doctors were telling him, and how he stood there now weary and saddened by the changes on the MRI. I watched him as he then looked past me through the open door of the room. He smiled when he caught site of his bride of 32 years and continued to watch her with a gentle look on his face. I turned my head toward her as well and saw her sitting in the room quietly, waiting for her prince to return.

Move Around It

Her smile lit up the room. Despite the fact that she had to plug up the breathing tube sticking out from her throat every time she wanted to speak. Despite her short breathy sentences that were bookended by gasps of air as every word came at the price of oxygen. Despite the permanent weakness in her legs that prevented her from getting up from a chair without first pushing herself up with her arms, carefully finding her balance and then using a wheeled walker to get around her house. Despite all the abnormal spots in her brain and spinal cord from the multiple sclerosis that landed her in the hospital at least once or twice a year. Despite all of this, she was the picture of joy.

She was a beautiful 41-year-old woman with bright eyes and the most positive attitude of any patient I'd seen in a long time. I had the privilege of taking care of her in the hospital for a few days while she was receiving treatment for a serious urinary tract infection. When I first met her, I asked her who took care of her at home. With a bit of sass, she shot back "I do." She told me that she and her husband had a daily routine. She moved slowly because of all her health issues, so she had to start cooking dinner at around 2:30 in the afternoon. By 5pm, she would have everything ready and her chores around the house done so that when her husband got home from work they could eat dinner together. As she put it, "Life doesn't stop when you get sick. I just move around it."

I love that. It's not a new idea that we have to learn to cope with what life deals us, but the way she said it put it in a different light. "I move around it" implies that, okay, so maybe this thing is too big for us to fight, to defeat or to ignore. It's a permanent part of our lives that will never go away, so we just go around it and keep on going. It's like a giant rock in our path that we cannot move and that forces us to take the long way around it. The journey is much harder and at times more painful, but we can still make it to our destination and maybe even enjoy ourselves along the way.

On the last day she was in the hospital, I told her what a wonderful and inspiring human being she was. She smiled and said, "No one promised me a good life, but I got a life."

I love that, too.

A Holy Man

One of my patients was a Secret Service agent who had been assigned to protect the likes of Condoleezza Rice, Nelson Mandela, and other notable political figures over the years. When I asked him what his favorite detail had been, he said it was protecting the Dalai Lama. Years ago, the agent and his colleagues had been assigned to guard the exiled Buddhist monk from Tibet for a week during one of his trips to the U.S.

On the first day of the assignment, the agents formed a protective line from the entrance of a lecture hall to a nearby elevator so that the spiritual leader could reach it safely amidst throngs of fans and journalists vying for his attention. When the Dalai Lama finally made it to the elevator, he saw my patient standing inside waiting for him with a stern, expressionless face. The Tibetan monk smiled warmly and then put both of his hands squarely on the burly agent's shoulders. "You are too serious," he said with a laugh.

Over the next few days, the agent was amazed by how kind and genuine the Dalai Lama was. When he asked one of the agents how he was doing, he really wanted to know. He really cared about them. And it showed in the way he spoke to the agents, the warmth in his gestures, and the genuine smile he had for all those men that would readily give their lives to protect his. He was grateful for their care and dedication, even it was just part of their job.

At the end of the week, all of the agents on that detail, regardless of their faith or religious background said, "Now *that* was one holy man."

The Blanche Dubois Syndrome

E ven as a child I was never partial to the story of the emperor's new clothes, the tale of a vain and foolish ruler who was tricked into thinking that he was wearing only the finest clothing when in fact he was completely nude. When my mother read it to me at night, I would cry out with frustration, "But he's naked! Why can't he see that?" For years, I identified with the child at the end of the story who finally pointed out that the emperor was indeed in the buff. It bothered me to no end when I would see people openly denying the truth or adulterating it for whatever reason, even if it was just to make things easier to swallow. I went so far as to create a diagnosis for people who knowingly ignored what was right in front of their eyes. I deemed them all to be suffering from the Blanche Dubois Syndrome after the histrionic character from the Tennessee Williams play, *A Streetcar Named Desire*.[8]

In the play, Blanche Dubois was an aging southern belle with a torrid past and a self-afflicted inability to face the truth. She was the portrait of a deluded and self-centered woman who did not earn my sympathies except at the end when she goes mad after a traumatic physical and psychological confrontation with her brother-in-law. For the most part though, I could not understand why anyone would ever want to be anything like her. For what could be worse than denying the truth? Little did I know at the time that it was the truth itself that could sometimes be too painful, too destructive for the human soul to bear.

But that all changed with the death of Iris Chang in 2004. An internationally known historian who wrote about war atrocities inflicted upon Chinese civilians by Japanese soldiers in her book, *The Rape of Nanking: The Forgotten Holocaust of World War II*, she was only 36 when she died.[9] After battling with severe depression for over a year, Chang shot herself in the head one morning in her car on the side of a California highway. She left behind a husband, a 2-year-old son and a glorious career.

I was stunned and heartbroken that one of my heroes was now gone and in such a horrible way. Chang was a young Asian-American woman who had broken all gender and racial barriers when she brought the Chinese holocaust into mainstream consciousness by writing a book that ended up on the New York Times bestseller list. More importantly, she had tracked down the survivors who had been forgotten by history and painstakingly documented their stories so that the world would never forget them again. She was an amazing individual who was a role model not only for Asian-Americans and women everywhere, but also for anyone who champions the rights of the poor, the wronged and those with no voice.

When a friend told me about her death, I went from website to website reading about her depression, the psychiatric hospitalizations and her suicide note that asked her friends and family to remember her as she was before she fell ill. Each click of the mouse brought me more stories of her despair and decline despite all of the doctors and pills and her best efforts to break out of her all-consuming depression. After a while, I was so profoundly saddened and so sorry for how much she must have suffered that I started to feel dazed and rather numb. So I did the only thing I could think of to do while staring at the computer screen. I surfed the web for new clothes.

I clicked mindlessly through fall clearance sales on sweaters. Buy one flimsy pink sweater, get another flimsy pink sweater for half off. It was a willed escape. I turned my head away from the *Rape of Nanking*, from the tragedy of Iris Chang's suicide. And that's when I realized we need Blanche Dubois. When the truth becomes so heavy that we can no longer breathe, sometimes all we can do is just close our eyes. As human beings, our capacity for self-deception may be limitless, but that's only because our capacity to suffer is finite. Once we reach a certain point, we simply break.

The Blanche Dubois Syndrome is all around us. We dye our hair when it starts turning gray or style it to hide the places where it's thinning. We wear makeup to cover our blemishes, slimming clothes with special fabrics to hold us in and keep things tucked away. Padded bras. Padded resumes. And then there are the more serious denials of a tormented childhood that is still without closure, a fractured marriage that makes us feel lonelier than if we were actually alone, a child or sibling who was once much loved but has now grown distant. Personal failures and deep regrets that we cannot yet reconcile are glossed over by manufactured social smiles and light, airy greetings that tell the world we're fine even if we're far from it. Because that's exactly what we need to tell ourselves to survive until we choose to face our fears head on and deal with them in the healthiest way possible.

We cannot underestimate the power of the Blanche Dubois Syndrome, nor should we take it lightly if we choose to pop the bubble or "cure" someone of their disease by confronting them with the truth whether it is out of malice or genuine concern for their well-being. To do so without committing ourselves to fully supporting these individuals and providing the necessary avenues for them to get the help they need would be to destroy another human being. We help no one when we force someone to face the truth too soon. Certainly, if someone we love is being abused or has an addiction to alcohol and drugs, then an intervention may indeed be necessary. But unless we are willing to follow it through to the level of care that is needed, then a more gentle approach with the help of other people should be considered.

The Blanche Dubois Syndrome is a necessary defense mechanism that in more dire situations is hopefully only temporary. When we see people who are afflicted with it, our first thought shouldn't be to point out the truth, but to have kindness for them. For underneath their elaborate charade there is a great deal of pain, a gaping hole that may never be filled. And the more elaborate the denial system, the deeper the suffering. Life is painful enough for them. There is no need to make it more so by taking away what may be their last fragile link to reality. It's not necessary to play along with them or reinforce the denial, but we should give these people compassion and help them if we can.

So the next time we see the emperor, we can just smile when he asks us what we think of his new clothes. Then offer him a jacket.

How to Give Bad News

There are three things in life that are overrated: French wine, extra-marital love affairs and fasciculations.

Author unknown

he first time I had to give bad news to someone that I had just met, things didn't go so well. When I walked into the clinic room that morning as a young resident, I could see that the patient and his wife were clearly VIPs. She was adorned with expensive jewelry, finely tailored clothing and the look — that unmistakable "how-dare-you-keep-us-waiting, don't-you-know-we-have-more-money-than-God" look. He was anxious, too, but did not greet me with the same icy glare. With my best smile, I tried to explain how the staff physician and I had been mistakenly overbooked that day and apologized profusely for their prolonged wait, not unlike an airline stewardess who had absolutely nothing to do with the plane's delay. They both calmed down considerably throughout the interview and turned out to be a very nice couple. He even smiled as he denied any muscle twitching, saying that he was completely healthy except for some mild difficulty buttoning his shirt.

He dutifully answered all of my questions . No, he did not smoke or take recreational drugs. Yes, he had a martini now and then. No, no one in his family had any neurological problems. Towards the end of the conversation, he mentioned that he was a retired Naval officer who had served in Korea and Vietnam. When I told him that I was also in the Navy and would be serving as a neurologist after I finished my training, his face lit up and he raised his hand to slap mine in a high-five motion. It was a connection, a shared experience that brought us together on equal ground away from the paternalism of the traditional doctor-patient relationship that in this case was imbalanced by the social dissonance of a yacht club member and a minimum-wage resident physician.

In medical school, a psychiatrist had once pointed out that medicine was the only occupation in which a complete stranger would remove his clothing simply on request. It was an odd truth that passed quickly through my mind as I asked him to undress for the physical examination. To my surprise, I found myself praying that this man would not have a terrible disease like ALS, a progressive disorder of the brain and spinal cord that is usually fatal within three to five years of diagnosis. But when he removed his shirt revealing a constant stream of muscle twitching that rippled underneath his skin from head to toe, I knew my prayers would not be answered.

"Um...do you see these twitches?" I asked almost sheepishly.

He casually looked down and said, "Oh yeah," as if he'd just discovered a bit of mustard he had spilled on his tie.

"Those muscle twitches are called fasciculations. They're not specific for any one disease and can be seen in normal people. But they can also be seen with different kinds of nerve and muscle problems like a pinched nerve in the neck or...Lou Gehrig's disease also known as ALS."

I was trying to be helpful and remained rather general in my statements until the staff physician arrived. He would have to be the one to deliver the final blow as I could not yet do it myself. I knew it was over for this man who had bravely served in two wars, worked his way up from salesman to CEO of his company and was now just beginning to enjoy the fruits of his life's labors.

I carefully but mechanically finished the examination, which revealed other indisputable signs of an incurable disease that would eventually rob him of his independence, his mobility and finally his breath. I shook his atrophied hand, the hand that had embraced mine as a kindred spirit only 20 minutes ago. My heart sank and I left the room in tears.

Many years have passed since that day, and I now give this diagnosis at least once or twice a week to patients from all over the world. Although I would never use a rehearsed speech for something so personal and so devastating, I learned how to approach these discussions from my mentor and friend Dr. Glen Stevens. As a brain tumor specialist at the Cleveland Clinic, Dr. Stevens has been the perpetual bearer of bad news for over 20 years.

In the world of theater, it's all about timing. But when it comes to giving patients a serious diagnosis, it's about how we first open the dialogue, because this is what sets the tone for everything that happens afterwards. As long as we are honest and compassionate, there's no right or wrong way to do things, but Dr. Stevens' opener is consistent and on point. He looks straight at the patient and asks, "How much do you want to know?" With that simple question, he manages to do two things. The first is that he gives patients control, which is something they haven't experienced since they first noticed things weren't quite right. The second thing is that he gives them an out, meaning they can simply opt to hear the information they are ready to receive and not a word more. For a number of people that's enough, because sometimes they just don't want to know.

They don't want to hear how much time they have left or what to expect as the tumor grows bigger. They don't want to see the films that show the large mass sitting in the middle of their brain. They're fine leaving the clinic with just a diagnosis and that's it. Because in reality they do know. By the time they come to see a specialist at a major medical center they know that what they have is bad, and they're not ready to process that. And that's okay. Everyone has his or her own way of dealing with things.

When I ask my ALS patients that same question, most of them say they want to know everything. Yet after I start talking for a few minutes, some of them will actually stop me mid-conversation, because it's too much too soon. Or their eyes start to glaze over while I'm telling them about breathing machines and feeding tubes. At that point I realize I'm like the teacher in the old Charlie Brown cartoons where the only thing the patients are hearing in between "bad news" and "you have ALS" is "wah wah wah wah." That's when I stop talking and give them some space.

Bad news can come from anyone, not just a physician. It can be from our accountant as when he lets us know that we won't be getting a tax refund this year and in fact we actually owe the IRS money. Or our boss who tells us that because of recent budget cuts in personnel we'll be working Thanksgiving and Christmas. And of course, bad news can come from someone we love. A friend of mine found out that her sister's beloved boyfriend of two years was married to another woman and had just had a baby with her. How he had kept it concealed from her sister for so long was unclear, but there had been signs ("just call me on my cell because my home phone is out of service") that had made my friend suspicious enough to start poking around through mutual friends and acquaintances. Her suspicions confirmed with actual photographs of the smiling family, my friend knew she had to tell her sister who had been patiently waiting for an engagement ring.

In these instances, timing is important. My friend waited until she and her sister were away on a girls' shopping weekend so that there would be some physical distance from the boyfriend and also so that the sister would have time to recover before she had to go back to work. Then like Dr. Stevens, my friend started out the conversation with a question, "I have something to tell you. Do you want to hear it now or wait until later?" There are times when people have other things on their plate to deal with, so if their heads are full and what we're about to tell them will not result in their immediate death or demise, then it may be better to wait until they're in the proper state of mind. As the two women were supposedly on a relaxing getaway, the sister didn't have anything else going on so she just looked at her strangely and said, "Tell me now."

My friend told her sister about the boyfriend and kept it very short and to the point. Stunned, her sister just stared at her in disbelief. After a few moments, she asked if she could call him. My friend nodded and told her to call the house phone, the one that was supposedly out of service. The sister dialed, the call went through and the boyfriend picked up on the other line. She was greeted by his voice and a baby's cries in the background. That was all she needed to hear. The only thing she managed to say was, "Why?" and then hung up vowing never to speak to him again. What my friend did next was probably the most important thing, and that was to be there for her sister. The weekend was rough as were the next several months, but the sister made it through and is now with a kind man who has been faithful and true in the years they've been together.

When we give someone bad news, we need to make sure that we're coming from a place of kindness, that the reason we are breaking the news is not to harm anyone or to show off that we are in the know, but to help the other person. Because if the news is bad and our intention is anything less than pure, not only will the person fail to appreciate us for telling her, but she may direct her anger and blame towards us even if we had nothing to do with it. We may also feel guilty because in effect we are hurting the other person with the information that we're giving her. If we're really trying to help, then everyone involved will understand that it's a necessary pain like ripping off a Band-Aid. But if we just want to be the one who breaks the news for our own ego, then the fact that we hurt another individual simply as a power trip will eventually come back to bite us in the end.

Another thing my friend did like Dr. Stevens was to give her sister a choice at the beginning. This is a crucial step as it shows respect for a person's right NOT to know, and lets her have time to let things slowly sink in as they will. That little bit of denial, the allowance of the Blanche Dubois Syndrome (see previous chapter), is necessary for some people so that they don't completely shut down. And finally, we have to be ready to comfort them. The news of her boyfriend's deceit could have ruined the sister for life in that she would never be able to trust another man again. But my friend found the right time to give her the news and was very careful in how she handled her sister. She let her cry it out that weekend and won a permanent spot at number one on her sister's speed dial.

Nobody likes to get bad news. Centuries ago, it was not uncommon to kill the poor messenger who brought forth unwanted news such as that about the approach of an enemy, the marriage of a beloved to another, or a tax increase. But if we have to be the ones who break the news, then we can do so with compassion, honesty and respect.

In the movie *Up in the Air*, George Clooney played a traveling consultant whose primary job was to fire people from different companies.[10] While the act of terminating someone's position after years of loyal service is itself cold and brutal, Clooney's character brought a human aspect to each encounter that softened the blow and in some cases gave the newly terminated employee hope. He would scan their resumes to see if there had been education or training in another field and then brought that up in conversation as something they could pursue again. He was open, sincere and gave them time to ask questions and air out their grievances.

The most poignant scenes of the movie though were not scripted nor were they shot with actors. The director interviewed real people who had been fired from their jobs, and asked them to reenact on camera what they had said and done on the day they had actually been let go. Some of them just sat there staring, while others started shouting, crying or throwing things. But what they had in common was that the thing that bothered them most about being fired was not the loss of their salaries, but the uncertainty of what was going to happen next.[11] The question many of them asked was: What am I supposed to do now? And that is what makes bad news so bad. Fear. It's the fear of the unknown, of being lost, alone, in pain or dying. When our sense of security and well-being is unexpectedly taken away from us, it's like we're suddenly standing in front of this huge void. Even if it lasts for just a moment, that feeling of not knowing what to do next can be absolutely terrifying.

If we keep that in mind the next time we have to tell people something that could potentially change their lives and not necessarily for the better, then we can prepare for it and do what we can to allay those fears when they arise. Depending on the person or situation, we can make gentle suggestions for what to do next or give them a very simple to-do list that they can carry out without having to dwell on all of the potential ramifications of what we just told them. Sometimes just being in the room with them afterwards lets them know that they are not alone, that they matter as a person, and that someone cares for them. We may have given them news that they didn't want to hear, but by being kind and sensitive we can sometimes give them what they need to heal.

Green Bananas

I f someone would have asked me a few years ago how many types of bananas there are in the world, I would have scratched my head in confusion and said, "You mean there's more than Chiquita?"*

At my mother's rainforest temple in Thailand, there are huge trees bearing bananas of various colors, sizes and flavors. My favorite are the Lady Fingers, which are very sweet and fit in the palm of my hand. Whenever I'm there for my annual meditation retreat, my mother will ask a local villager to cut down a bunch of Lady Fingers from one of the trees just for me. I'll eat them for breakfast, snacks and sometimes even for dinner. It's hard to find that specific variety of banana in the U.S. so it's something that I really enjoy when I'm there, especially when they're picked right off the tree.

*Chiquita is the #1 selling brand of bananas in the U.S. and markets the Cavendish variety in supermarkets across the country. It is not a type of banana.

One year, I went for my meditation retreat a little earlier in the fruit season than usual. When I arrived at the temple, there was a giant bunch of bananas sitting on the front porch waiting for me. The problem, though, was that none of them was even close to being ripe as evident by their dark green color. For the first few days, I glared at the bananas with contempt and the patience of a 2-year-old child as they sat on the porch taunting me with their defiantly green skin. I then started to get a little anxious as each day that passed without a change in their color added to the growing possibility that I would return to the States without having had the pleasure of eating just one. When almost a week had gone by and they still weren't ready, I realized I had a choice. I could just rip one open and eat it out of spite, knowing that it wouldn't taste very good and would probably give me a stomachache to boot. Or I could continue waiting until they were properly ripened and just accept the fact that if they were still green by the time I had to leave, I'd simply go back to the good old Chiquita bananas from my local grocery store when I returned home.

In that moment when I made up my mind to let things happen as they would, I felt an internal release of tension. I didn't forget about the Lady Fingers nor did I give up on waiting for them to ripen; I just decided that I would be fine either way. With that, I could walk by the porch without feeling irritated and my sense of entitlement faded away as did that subconscious anger that comes with unmet expectations. Even my meditation seemed a little better. In the last two days of my trip, the bananas found their golden hue and I was able to enjoy the sweet fragrant taste of my Lady Fingers. But even if it hadn't worked out, my only regret would be that I had wasted that first week fretting over something so silly as a bunch of bananas.

We may not always get what we want, but we always have a choice in how we deal with it. Of course we're not happy when the prospect of getting what we want slips away from us before our very eyes, but we can choose to be bitter and angry about it or we can acknowledge that sometimes things don't work out and just move on. Yes, when we're in the thick of things it's difficult to see that there is indeed a choice when all we can see is our own misery. But if we step back from the situation for a moment, as I did with the bananas and look at what all that drama is doing to us, then it becomes clear that there's no benefit in getting upset. In fact it only hurts us, which makes everything worse.

Once we understand this, then we can make a conscious decision to walk away from all the emotional baggage we've attached to our desire and learn to be okay with the way things are. The funny thing is that when we've made the decision to accept the outcome whatever it may be, we sometimes end up getting what we want at the last minute. Not only that, but we appreciate it more.

Part of the reason may be that the very nature of expectation creates a mindset that leads us to take things for granted. If the bananas had been ripe, I would have simply eaten them without giving it a second thought. But because I had to wait for them and was faced with the possibility that I would have to go another year without even tasting one, their value increased in my mind and I enjoyed eating them that much more. In a way, it's a win-win situation when we let things go. It's even better when we get what we want, but we're perfectly okay if we don't.

Certainly, there are bigger things in life that we may want or actually need, and it's not easy to just walk away when things don't go as we'd hoped. In those cases, we may have to look for alternatives, backup options or just wait things out. But there are so many little things in our daily lives that we can learn to let go, which in turn helps us establish a healthier way of thinking that can be applied to more important things later on.

So whenever life hands us green bananas, the real issue isn't about whether or not they will ripen in time for us to eat them, but how we decide to think and act if they don't. We have to remember that we always have a choice, and hopefully we'll choose wisely.

Too Much of a Good Thing

E very day is a bad hair day for me in Thailand. Whenever I'm there visiting relatives, I often look like I just rolled out of bed as the dense humidity causes much of my hair to frizz out in random directions, while the rest of it is matted down to my sweaty head. Born and raised in Illinois where I've always enjoyed the four seasons, I can't see myself ever getting used to the 100+ degree heat of my ancestors' homeland. But according to human biology, my body is preprogrammed to do just. Adaptation to weather, geography and pain has been key to man's survival since the beginning of time.

Our bodies are constantly adapting to the world around us. For instance, when we walk into a room and there's a strong smell of garbage or heavy perfume, something happens inside the brain and after a while the smell doesn't bother us anymore. We get used to it and may even come to like it. When my father first came to the U.S., he'd never had cheese before and threw up the first time he ate pizza. For the first couple of years, he couldn't even stand the smell of it. Now he gets his super deluxe pizza with Parmesan cheese sprinkled all over it.

On the flipside, adaptation limits our sense of pleasure. I once read somewhere that the enjoyment we get from taking that first bite of a delicious meal goes away by the fourth bite. It's the same principle as when we experience something unpleasant, like a bad odor, loud background noise or in my father's case the taste of cheese. After a while, the brain's receptors learn to adapt so that the sensation, be it pleasant or unpleasant, eventually levels off. This is the basic foundation for drug addiction. There's a brief period of pleasure, but after it goes away more of the drug is needed to reproduce or sustain that initial high. Addicts then have to do all sorts of things to get more drugs, which results in a vicious downward spiral. While most of us don't fall into that category, the principle of adaption applies to the pursuit of any type of pleasure. This can lead to multiple problems, especially when we devote a significant amount of our lives trying to fulfill our desires.

Howard Hughes was one of the richest men in the 20th century. He was also one of the strangest. An eccentric billionaire whose later life was marred by mental illness and an addiction to pain medications, Hughes was a prime example of unlimited desire gone awry, as his massive wealth allowed him to indulge his every whim. While living at the Desert Inn in Las Vegas, Hughes developed a penchant for Banana Nut ice cream and ate it every single day.[12] When his personal assistants saw that the hotel's supplies were running low, they moved heaven and earth to get the Baskin-Robbins ice cream company to make a new batch just for him, even though the flavor had already been discontinued. Once the ice cream was made, it was quickly driven through the California desert in a refrigerated truck so that it could be stored in a special freezer in the hotel. However, on the very night that the ice cream arrived, Hughes announced that he was switching to French Vanilla. Just like that. The hotel was stuck with 350 gallons of Banana Nut ice cream for years.

When the thrill of a pleasant sensation wears off, our interests shift and we have to find something else to entertain us. The mind can't stand to be still or bored. It requires constant stimulation and always seeks out new things to capture its attention. If we allow the mind to chase after each desire, we'll enter into a never-ending cycle like the poor drug addict who spends his life trying to score more drugs so he can keep getting high until he finally crashes. While a desire for something like Banana Nut ice cream isn't as destructive as cocaine, the principle is the same. The mind will never be at peace. Going from one desire to another was a recurring theme in Howard Hughes' life. Despite being able to get almost every material thing he wanted, Hughes was an unhappy man who eventually died alone and in squalor.

Another thing that happens when we start enjoying something is that not only do we get accustomed to it, but also whatever it is that brought us pleasure becomes a must-have, a maintenance level that we expect and then demand later on. Whenever we experience anything less, we easily become upset or unhappy. It can be a certain type of lotion, a brand of cereal or even an internet speed that we simply can't do without. This extends to our personal comfort as well. The first time we are upgraded to first class on an airplane, we're wowed by the large leather seats and the warmed nuts served before takeoff. But on the way back when our knees and elbows are crammed into an economy class seat, the discomfort is magnified and we long for the attentive service that's often lacking back in the cattle car.

Our expectations for personal comfort aren't always for something super luxurious. Even the simple flush toilet, which is the standard in Western bathrooms, is unfortunately not a universal item. My friends and I learned this when we were on a road trip through the Moroccan countryside years ago. As with all long car rides, eventually some of us had to use the restroom. We stopped at a little gas station where we were led to a small foul-smelling room with a primitive squat toilet on the floor and no toilet paper. My friends had let me go first as I had been the one to request the pit stop, but as soon as I saw the very non-Western and non-sanitary appearing commode, I made an immediate U-turn and told my friends who were waiting outside for me that I would just hold it. My friend who was driving said that we didn't have time to stop again; otherwise we'd miss the ferry back to Spain. After a brief discussion and some encouragement from my other friends, I went back in. Flustered, I did my best balancing act and ended up urinating all over myself.

In reality, the flush toilet and many other things that we take for granted here in the U.S. are actually considered to be luxury items in less developed areas around the world. In relative terms, our barometers at baseline are already set at a high level, but with adaptation we constantly reset it at even higher levels whenever we want and expect more. Yet, this doesn't bring us more happiness. And it certainly doesn't make us better people. In fact, it can change us for the worse.

It's estimated that we have about 60,000 thoughts a day, of which 90% were the same as the day before.* As most of these thoughts are undoubtedly centered on various aspects of our lives — what we want, how we feel, what happened in our past — it's safe to say that most people think about themselves nearly all of the time. In some respects, thoughts related to the self and how we function in the world are a natural part of our existence. But endless navel-gazing and thoughts focused on ensuring our comfort and pleasure are not necessary for our survival. Over time, these thoughts may evolve into an established pattern of thinking that we apply to all aspects of our lives. It can change us, making us more self-centered, vain, and aggressive. Our lives and our agendas start to mean more than anything else, and slowly that becomes evident in all of our interactions.

When we talk to people, we stop listening to what they're saying as we're only interested in making our own thoughts and ideas known. When we're driving, we become angered by anything that stands in the way of our destination. Red lights, rush hour traffic or slow moving cars can actually enrage us. It also affects the way we see others. The people around us cease to be fellow human beings who have hopes and fears just as we do. Instead, they're seen as obstacles, competitors or tools that we can use to our benefit. If they don't fall into one of these categories, then we don't see them at all. They simply don't exist for us. It's said that a man's true character is revealed in how he treats people he thinks are of no use to him.

The more we engage in behaviors and activities that revolve solely around the fulfillment of our desires, the more isolated we become. While we may indeed get all the things that we want, it comes at the price of intense loneliness. This is because when

*Attributed to Dr. Fred Luskin, a Stanford psychologist

we are so focused on ourselves, we stop caring about others. And when that happens, we start to feel empty. It doesn't matter how many friends we have or how many people love us. We don't feel connected. We don't feel anything. It's a state of being that is sometimes worse than death.

The antidote is to think of others. If we take a moment to look outside of ourselves, we will start to see how the people around us are in need or in pain. There are so many things we can do to help them, not by writing a check, but by listening, caring and wishing them well or at least not thinking ill of them. This pulls us out of our isolation and brings us into the present moment where we can feel that we are a part of something bigger than ourselves. When we are no longer wrapped up in our own thoughts and desires, those things that we wanted and thought that we absolutely needed to make us happy just don't seem that important anymore.

In Mother Teresa's book, *No Greater Love*, she tells the story of how one of the wealthy volunteers at her center in Calcutta loved expensive saris and would wear them to the center.[13] The volunteer's elegant dresses stood out in striking contrast to their modest surroundings and the poverty of the people they were serving. The wise nun guessed that the woman's saris cost upwards of 800 rupees compared to her own simple dress that cost only 8 rupees. So she told the woman that the next time she went out to buy a sari, she should buy one that cost only 500 rupees and then spend the other 300 rupees on saris for the poor. Not long after that, the woman came to understand the true spirit of giving and selflessness, and started wearing saris that cost 100 rupees, but only because Mother Teresa wouldn't let her buy anything cheaper.

The act of giving changed this woman's life. When she went from buying expensive saris for her own pleasure and vanity to that of providing clothing for the poor, she experienced pure joy, one that didn't fade over time and need to be replaced by yet another expensive dress. Giving cultivates empathy and compassion, which in turn inspires us to do even more for others. This is what brings meaning to our lives and over time can fulfill us in ways that all the luxury and material comfort in the world will never be able to do.

That's not to say that we suddenly need to give up the little luxuries that comfort us and help us cope with the stress of everyday life. But we can learn to enjoy them in small amounts and once we satisfy that initial craving, we stop indulging ourselves before adaptation kicks in and our sensation of pleasure naturally plateaus. For instance, if we only eat a piece of chocolate cake once in a while, it becomes something to look forward to and we can savor it to the last bite. But if we eat it every day, not only would we start to take for granted its rich, sweet taste, we may eventually grow tired of it.

Adaptation is built into our genetic makeup and is a necessary part of our lives. It allows us to survive under different physical and mental conditions, but just as it limits our pain so, too, does it limit our pleasure. We cannot change our biology, but we can stop resetting the barometer and learn how to be happy with what we have by looking beyond our own desires, thinking of others and giving more of ourselves. The result is a sense of peace that fills us from within, transcending pleasure and all adaptive mechanisms.

bloom

The Invisible Tiger

I t's interesting how the things we think will bring us happiness often fall short of our expectations. But the things we think will be painful rarely disappoint us. It's like when we drop something heavy on our foot and there's that split second right before our brain registers the sensation of a million smashed nerves in our toe. We may not feel anything at first, but we know it's going to hurt. So when the sharp burst of pain shoots through our foot, it's exactly how we thought it would be, if not worse.

When we're hit with an obvious source of pain, be it a physical injury or an emotionally charged event, we have an idea of what's in store for us down the line. If there's enough leeway, we can even prepare for it or at least recognize that there's something hurting us so that we can treat it appropriately as needed. Each day, however, we experience more subtle forms of pain that don't seem like a big deal at the time, but can hurt us later on in ways we never imagined. It can be a brief twinge of jealousy when a coworker gets a promotion, the nail-biting anxiety of waiting for something we have no control over, or the sting of anger when things don't work out the way we'd hoped. Along with hatred, greed, fear and depression, these negative mental states can be damaging even in small doses. The great Buddhist scholar Ajahn Buddhadasa once likened these destructive thoughts of the mind to a tiger that would readily devour us the moment we let down our guard.

The problem is that most of us can't see this tiger. It's an invisible predator that appears out of nowhere, and yet it's always there, nipping at us, biting us and sometimes, badly hurting us. We look down and suddenly we see all these scratch marks on our bodies or huge open wounds where it took a giant bite out of our flesh. Similarly, dark and unhealthy thoughts can bring us down in an instant or cause us to suddenly feel tense, lonely, or afraid seemingly out of the blue. The worst part of it is that because we're not able to see the tiger (most people don't even know that it exists), we can live our entire lives letting it hurt us at will. We become a constant victim of the tiger — of our own thoughts — without knowing that there is actually something we can do about it.

The way to defeat the tiger is through mindfulness. Like our negative thoughts, the tiger is powerful. Most of us are not strong enough to fight it outright, and we can't just wish it away. So we have to build a cage around the tiger, guard it and then starve it until it eventually dies. Likewise, we must maintain constant vigilance of the mind and its movements by practicing mindfulness, and then stop feeding our negative thoughts by ruminating over what's already happened, trying to relive the past or being self-absorbed.

For some of us, the idea of mindfulness may be intimidating if we think of it as some sort of strict meditation practice in which we're sitting uncomfortably on the floor for prolonged periods of time in quiet torture. But mindfulness is just being aware of the fact that each thought that comes into the mind is just a thought. It's not real, and may not even be true. It's a creation of the mind that is completely separate from us and can be let go. For instance, whenever we find ourselves thinking about how someone was rude to us the day before, we have to recognize that the memory of that person's behavior is just a thought, and then let it go right there. Otherwise, it will quickly turn into a chain of thoughts. A simple memory of being slighted escalates when we start remembering how angry we were at what that person said to us and how mean she was when she said it. We go on to generate new thoughts about what we should have said in return followed by all of these plans about what we'll do the next time we see her. On and on, this chain of thoughts is what feeds the tiger, and it's what we have to stop.

In the beginning, it's helpful to start a formal sitting practice to first calm the mind so that we're not bombarded by numerous thoughts competing for our attention all at the same time. But once we start doing this regularly, mindfulness can be practiced any time — while we're walking down the street, driving a car to work or cooking dinner at home. When a thought pops into our head we acknowledge it and let it go. That's it. By stopping the chain of thoughts or preventing it from starting at all, we stop feeding the tiger so that we can eventually defeat it.

Many years ago, a friend of mine in the U.S. Navy was given a two-year duty assignment in Okinawa, Japan as a junior officer shortly after graduating from the Naval Academy. The small, quiet island was far away from home, and its culture and language were vastly different from what he was used to. He didn't want to be there as he missed his friends and family back in the U.S., but that's where had been assigned for the next two years. (There's a saying in the Navy — if you take the paycheck twice a month, you go where you're told.) In the first few months of moving there, he felt lonely and started to slip into a bit of depression. But before things got out of hand, he stopped himself and said, "I am not going to do this. I will not let myself get down about this."

He fought the tiger with everything he had. He practiced meditation, exercised religiously, worked in his garden and took long swims in the ocean. After a while he was able to capture the tiger and then conquer it. He grew to love the island. He learned how to speak very basic Japanese, became a huge fan of sushi and was an avid shopper at the 100 yen store, which is like the places here in the U.S. where everything's only a dollar. He finished his tour there with commendations from his superior officer and returned to the U.S. with a positive state of mind that he continues to maintain in every situation.

For some of us, there are many tigers that we have to fight. We all have layers of dark thoughts that we bury in order of how much they hurt us, the most painful being the ones we bury the deepest. Each tiger, each thought that we defeat leads to a bigger, more ferocious one until we face the most powerful of them all. And if we defeat this one, there is nothing we cannot handle. In the moments before he was to become enlightened, the Buddha was tempted by the evil forces of Mara* who brought forth beautiful women to entice him away from his quest for enlightenment. When that failed to move him, Mara tried to antagonize him with guilt by accusing

Mara is the demon in Buddhist literature that is similar to Satan in Judeo-Christian writing.

him of leaving his responsibilities as a father, a husband and an heir to the throne when he left his life in the palace to seek the truth. But the Buddha remained steadfast and was able to overcome Mara and the defilements of his mind, thus entering a state of enlightenment. It is believed by some that Mara is not a separate embodiment of evil, but like the tiger is actually another metaphor for our own personal demons. It's that little voice that urges us to do something we know isn't right, inspires fear or makes us feel small or jealous in comparison to another. Whether or not we believe that there is a real force of evil out there somewhere, we have enough to deal with as it is in our very own minds.

To keep the minds healthy, we must keep vigilant of our tigers and continue fighting them like a video game in which we advance to higher levels after defeating one tiger after another. Each time we master a level, we acquire new powers: more concentration, more inner strength, more wisdom and insight — all of which we need to fight in the next level until we reach the final one where, after defeating our most powerful tiger, whatever it may be, we can claim the ultimate victory.

bloom

Why We Love the Underdog

I was once asked to see a hospital patient whose vitamin B12 deficiency was so severe that it left her unable to walk and almost blind in both eyes. The MRI of her spinal cord was also abnormal and showed white spots along its entire length from her neck down to the lower back. Fortunately, she improved after receiving B12 injections and was eventually able to walk again with a walker. The case was memorable for how profoundly weak this woman had become from an untreated vitamin deficiency. But what I will also remember from this case was the attending physician who had consulted me for help.

I'd never met him before, and when I first walked into the room I saw him talking to the patient about all of the upcoming tests they had ordered for her while gently holding her hand. Within a few minutes of listening to the conversation, I could see how caring he was and also how deaf. He was a relatively young man, but wore hearing aids in both ears and had that unmistakable slurred speech of someone who had never been able to hear his own voice. In the brief time we met at the patient's bedside, he seemed compassionate and good-natured. Later on, when I discussed the case with him on the phone, he was again kind and expressed his gratitude for my help. But there was something else about him that hit a tender spot for me. I couldn't help but think of how he hard he must have worked to have come this far. It occurred to me that the importance of being able to hear is something we always took for granted in medical school when it came to all the lectures, our training in how to use a stethoscope, and the listening skills we need when talking to patients so that we can figure out what's wrong with them. I can't imagine how challenging it must have been for him, all the obstacles that he had to overcome just to get through school not to mention residency training.

Throughout his life, there must have been some unkind people who probably made fun of him or said that he could never be a doctor because he was deaf. It brought to mind Derrick Coleman, the Seattle Seahawks football player whose climb to the National Football League as the first deaf offensive player was anything but easy. After years of being teased and dismissed, of being told that he could never make it to the NFL because of his hearing impairment, he proved them all wrong and now sports a Super Bowl championship ring. His story was briefly featured in a poignant television commercial that has been known to bring even grown men to tears.

Another individual with a similar story is the singer Paul Potts who became internationally famous as the winner of a televised talent show in England years ago. Although he wasn't deaf, he was severely bullied for much of his life at first for being poor and then just for being different. With his broken teeth and shy demeanor, he won the hearts of the show's judges, the crowd and the entire world when he sang Puccini's "Nessun Dorma" on national television. His video performance and the audience's standing ovation is one of the most viewed internet videos of all time.

Despite all of their adversities, these individuals kept going and put in everything they had, working two if not three times harder than everyone else to achieve their goals. Fortunately, they succeeded and were able to enjoy the fruits of their labor. But what touches us most is not so much that they overcame their impairments to make their dreams a reality (although we do admire that), it was that throughout out their lives they were ridiculed, left out and left behind. Yet, they didn't give up. They fought on and remained humble without a visible chip on their shoulder. In the end, when the time was right they got their day in the sun. And that is what moves us, because at one point in our own lives we've all felt small, unwanted or forgotten even if it was just for a brief moment in time. We know what that feels like. When we see them, we see ourselves.

But there's something else about their stories that pull us in. It's a quality that's almost intangible. It's not just happiness for their success nor is it simply a shared sense of victory because we see ourselves in them. There's something deeper about seeing a person who was considered a nobody his entire life, a human being who has always been mistreated or ignored finally get recognized for the wonderful person that he really is. It's a profound sense of redemption that is good and pure and real. It's as if we all touch a state of grace by the sheer fact that we are there to witness it. And that is why we love the underdog.

bloom

24-Hour Time Travel

T ime travel has been the subject of many movies. Going back in time to try and change the course of events, like rescuing a loved one from death, is a very popular theme. Traveling into the future is also interesting and can make for fun science fiction movies. A less exciting but more fascinating concept is when time is limited to one particular day that's repeated over and over again. By some fluke of nature or magic spell, the movie's main character keeps waking up on the same exact day experiencing the same sequence of events. It's not as sexy or entertaining as the other themes, but it's a more accurate representation of the repetitive nature of our everyday lives.

In the movies *Groundhog Day* and *Edge of Tomorrow: Live, Die, Repeat* the main characters are initially shown to be selfish and self-centered individuals who have very little if any redeeming qualities.[14,15] But because they have to relive the same day repeatedly throughout the course of the film, they eventually learn to get it right. Before they come to that realization though, they do everything they can to game the system or escape the situation. In *Groundhog Day* the actor Bill Murray plays a vain weather forecaster who experiences Groundhog Day ad nauseam while stuck in a small town. In the beginning, he figures out what's going to happen at every minute. So he steals money from a bank, gorges himself on unhealthy food, and seduces a woman by convincing her he will marry her the following day knowing full well that the next day is not going to come anytime soon. In *Edge of Tomorrow*, Tom Cruise is a smooth-talking army officer who is more of a publicity agent rather than a true soldier. When his ugly cowardice becomes apparent, he's thrown into boot camp where he is stripped of his rank and abused by his fellow enlisted soldiers. But because of an alien time loop, he has to relive that painful day repeatedly. At first he tries to convince everyone of what's happening to him so that they will let him go. When that doesn't work, he becomes an army deserter and rides a stolen motorcycle into town to drink himself into oblivion. After a while, the main characters in both movies start to see that indulging in worldly pleasures doesn't help their cause nor does it bring them any happiness.

Eventually, they become weary of the entire experience and finally start to accept things for what they are. They change for the better and become selfless, thereby breaking the spell. With all of the time that's been forced upon him, Bill Murray stops focusing on himself and helps the people around town, takes piano lessons and learns how to carve ice sculptures. Tom Cruise trains to become an expert combat fighter, battles all the aliens and in his last gesture sacrifices himself to save the human race. At the end of both movies, the characters wake up to find that time is finally linear again and that they made it to a new day.

When the characters are trapped in a time loop, to some extent that's what life in the modern world is like. We wake up and go about our routine — work, school, running errands, taking care of the kids and the house. Then we come home, have dinner, put the kids to bed, do a little work around the house, go to sleep and then do the same thing again the next day. There are variations, of course, but for the most part the overall pattern is the same. Some people may be just fine with that and are content with the way things are. But others may find the routine tiresome and think that there has to be something more, that something is missing. They go through the motions each day and do what they're supposed to do, but in a joyless manner that's punctuated by bouts of unhappiness, stress or anxiety. There may be meaning in the little things they do, but in the grand scale of things sometimes it all seems rather pointless.

Granted, this routine would be a blessing for many people living in third-world countries or war-torn regions where clean water, personal safety and an adequate food supply are all daily concerns. But Mother Teresa who dedicated her life to helping the poorest of the poor recognized that the West with all of its money and material goods has the spiritually poorest of the poor. In her book *No Greater Love* she describes how it was much easier to give help to the hungry and homeless than to those with loneliness and anger in their hearts.[13] That doesn't mean that a boring routine automatically equals bitterness, but a feeling of emptiness and discontentment could be considered a form of spiritual hunger as well.

So when we feel like we're stuck in a routine, we can think of ourselves as those characters in a time loop and see each new day as another opportunity to learn and improve ourselves. It is a more difficult route to be sure, one that takes self-reflection, effort and determination. And if we think that we're too busy to change or are uncomfortable venturing from our routine at this time, then we can always choose to stay the same. But then life will stay the same.

On the other hand, if we take the time to learn from our mistakes and consciously try to be a kinder and more giving person — not just for our own family, but also for our neighbors, friends and community as a whole — then things can and will be different. Over time, we'll experience a gradual but noticeable change within ourselves that affects the way we think, our interactions with others and how we perceive the world around us. When we start directing our attention away from ourselves and toward helping others, we start to feel lighter. Our minds are clearer and we can see through problems easier. The discontentment and emptiness begin to fade away and are eventually replaced by a sense of fulfillment. Even if our actual routine remains the same, it is our minds that will change for the better. And like the characters in the movies, in the end we'll wake up to a new day and a new life.

A Wrong Turn

Love with hunger does not last.

Venezuelan proverb

In New York City where billion dollar deals are made over fine wine and a perfectly cooked steak, there is no shortage of swanky restaurants that cater to those with unlimited expense accounts. Fortunately, there are many other places in the city where the rest of us, the not-so-rich-and-powerful can dine on soupy Shanghai dumplings, Ethiopian sponge bread and other wonderful fare from all over the world without breaking the bank. The best places are usually small, family-owned restaurants that are hidden away in some forgotten corner of the city, like the Malaysian restaurant that my friend had chosen for dinner one evening while I happened to be in town.

The friend I was visiting was a kind and brilliant physician who had recently moved to the city to work for an international health organization. He'd suffered a nervous breakdown years ago after a tumultuous relationship ended quite badly, but had pulled his life together and was now remarried to a quiet young woman he'd met while working in Korea. After their wedding, she gave up her career as an editor in Seoul and followed him to New York where they seemed happy in their new life together.

It was a beautiful fall evening and we decided to walk to the restaurant from their apartment in midtown. The husband walked ahead of us chatting away with another one of our friends that he'd not seen for years, while the wife and I walked at a slower pace about a block behind them. Engrossed in what appeared to be a lively conversation, the two men didn't realize that they had missed the street where they were supposed to turn right. The woman called out to her husband to stop and turn around, but he could not hear her above the noisy traffic. Instead of calling out to him again, she just continued walking behind them without saying another word. I was puzzled that she didn't make another attempt to get his attention as they clearly needed to turn around, especially as our reservation was in danger of being given away if we were more than 15 minutes late. But I didn't want to be rude or overstep my boundaries as their guest so I just kept walking with her in the wrong direction.

We quickened our pace and eventually caught up with the men a couple blocks later at a stoplight. In a normal voice free of irritation, anger or sarcasm, she said we had missed the turn and needed to go back. That was it. No drama from either her or her husband. No mention that we were late for our reservation. Just a plainly spoken statement indicating we needed to turn around. So that's what we did. We traced our steps back, made the turn that we'd originally missed and arrived at the restaurant no worse for wear. We had a lovely meal accompanied by insightful discussions about love, politics, and life in the city. And other than that little navigational hiccup it was a perfect evening.

Several days later, I was still thinking about how smoothly everything had gone that night. I was so impressed by how my friend's wife had handled the situation and how calm she had remained even though we were running late for our reservation. A number of women I know would have yelled at their husbands to turn around immediately and would have kept yelling until they did. Or once they were able to catch up to their husbands, they'd be furious with them. This would be followed by a tense and unpleasant exchange, the kind that makes people witnessing such a glimpse of their married friends' private lives stare down at the floor or try to make a quick exit. But there had been none of that. It had all been very peaceful.

I later asked my mother what that was. What happened there? The woman exuded a quality that I couldn't put my finger on, something that I wanted to learn so I could be like that for myself and for others. Was it gentleness? Kindness?

My mother smiled and said it was patience.
Patience? Really?

That would never have crossed my mind. But my mother was right. A large part of patience is accepting things the way they are without getting angry or upset because it's not how we want them to be. It's a form of letting go, of letting things just be. When the man failed to make the turn, the wife knew that it was just a matter of time before he would figure it out himself or that we'd eventually catch up to him and let him know. And if we had never made it to that restaurant, it would have been fine. We would have just eaten somewhere else. There was nothing at stake, no harm done and certainly nothing worth getting upset over. The woman loved her husband and knew she had to be patient with him given his history. So when he made a mistake, she only tried to correct him once and then let him enjoy being with his friend. Her only concern that evening and maybe even for their marriage in general was her husband's happiness.

Although I'm not quite sure I would have done the same thing if I'd been in her shoes, it made me think that when we love someone with pure selflessness and compassion, perhaps the best thing we can really ask for is their happiness.

Beyond Main Street

I
n the 1998 movie *Pleasantville* a teenage boy and his older sister are magically transported back into time to a 1950s television show where everything around them is literally black and white.[16] They find themselves in a perfect idealized version of small-town America where the weather is perpetually 72 degrees and the most dangerous thing that happens all day is that a cat gets stuck in a tree. It's very far from reality and there's no depth or emotion to any of the smiling townspeople who are as blank as the empty pages of the school's library books. As the story progresses, the town starts to transform and little by little bits of color start to appear in the movie. In the most memorable scene, the teenage boy and his girlfriend slowly drive down a tree-lined street to the strains of Ella Fitzgerald crooning "At Last" from the car radio. Beautiful pink blossoms slowly fall from the branches above them, lingering in the air like jeweled snowflakes against a black-and-white background. It's dramatic, poetic and to borrow James Joyce's phrase it induces the soul to swoon.[17]

A less stunning but more insightful part of the movie is the classroom scene in which a high school geography teacher stands at the chalkboard and lectures on where Elm Street and Main Street intersect on a map of the town. The older sister finds this inane discussion ridiculous and asks the teacher what exists outside of Pleasantville. The teacher is dumbfounded and a little annoyed that anyone would want to know what was outside of their world. The other kids groan at her question and start whispering amongst themselves. Unfazed, the sister goes on to ask what lies at the end of Main Street, to which the teacher replies in all seriousness, "Well, it goes back to the beginning." The other students nod their heads in agreement, but the sister refuses to play along and remains defiant in her quest for knowledge.

What struck me about this scene was the sister's complete indifference to being ridiculed in front of the entire class. Many of us would have been embarrassed to have people saying unkind things about us behind our backs. Some of us may even have been humiliated if an authority figure showed our peers how irritating we were to her. We'd shrink down in our chairs and wish we could just disappear. But the sister didn't care and paid no attention to the other people's reactions toward her. Not because she was oblivious or aloof, but because she knew she was in an alternate universe, a black-and-white world that wasn't real. All of it was an illusion — the classroom, the empty books, and of course the meaningless idle chatter. She knew there was more to the world than just Main Street and most importantly, she knew who she was as a person. At the end of the movie, she discovered a newfound passion for learning and ended up staying in the alternate 1950s world to pursue a higher education.

Imagine how much easier life would be if, like the sister in the film, we could let go of what other people think about us and not take it to heart. Granted, the stakes were low in her case as she knew that she was in an artificial setting. But we don't have to be in an alternate universe to understand that other people's opinions about us don't really matter very much if at all. If we can accept who we are and understand that the world is so much bigger than a classroom, a workplace or an entire city, then it becomes apparent that the only thing that does matter is what we think about ourselves.

My friend's son has always been an exceptionally kind and affectionate child. When he was only 5-years-old, his teachers invited him to join an integrated classroom with special needs students to serve as a role model, tutor and friend. He loved being with all the different kinds of children, and his sunny disposition helped contribute to a warm and open atmosphere. But there's something else about him, too. He's comfortable in his own skin and doesn't care about what other people say about him. Although he's now 10, he still holds his father's hand to cross the street even in front of his friends, simply because he wants to. When he was younger, he used to be ashamed of a large birthmark on his side. He would cover it with a swim shirt at the pool so that the other kids wouldn't make fun of him. My friend and his wife never said anything about it or made him take it off because they didn't want him to feel bad, but one day he just stopped wearing the shirt at swim practice. When my friend asked him what changed his mind, he said, "Well, Dad, that's me. That's who I am." The kids still teased him for a bit, but he shrugged it off and kept swimming. And that's what we have to do. If there is something about us that we can't change or don't need to change, then that's us. That's who we are. We just have to accept it and move on.

Acceptance of who we are is an important step in building self-confidence. But it doesn't mean that we are settling for less. Rather, it's an objective self-reflection that gives us room to improve or stay the same as we choose. Acceptance is saying to ourselves and the world, "this is who I am right now," without adding any judgment to it. Settling, on the other hand, is when we think of ourselves as subpar or inferior in some way, and give up any hope of changing even though we're unhappy. This reinforces our negative thoughts and creates even more distance between who we are and who we want to be. Now if we want to change ourselves and we're able to, then that's fine. But we don't have to put ourselves down in the process.

For instance if we are a few pounds over what we should be for our age and height, acceptance is when we simply see that we're not at our ideal weight. We can take it a step further with a plan to diet and exercise, (which can make us feel better physically and mentally), or we can tell ourselves that we're okay with how we look and not give it another thought. Settling is when we think we're fat and unattractive, that we're stuck like this forever because we'll never be able to lose weight no matter what we do. There's a big difference in the two types of thought processes. The first has a neutral or even positive effect on our self-esteem, while the second has the power to destroy it. The good news is that we always have a choice as to which way we want to think about things.

With acceptance, we'll start to feel more confident. And with confidence, we can overcome fear. We will feel stronger about who we are as a person and will no longer be afraid of making mistakes in front of others. If we're strong enough, we may even look foolish on purpose or accept the blame if it's to help another human being in need. Some people will take responsibility and a verbal thrashing from their boss if their coworker, whose job is on the line, makes a mistake at work. Or a child will confess to something his little brother did to protect him from being punished.

I once heard a story about former First Lady Eleanor Roosevelt that I have yet to corroborate with official references, but love nonetheless. One evening during the 1930s, President Roosevelt and his wife invited several foreign dignitaries and members of the powerful elite to a formal White House dinner. As they sat discussing world politics over an exquisitely set table, a woman seated near the First Lady knocked over a glass of red wine onto the white linen tablecloth. Mortified by her social blunder at such an elegant event, the woman froze in her seat unable to say a word. The First Lady saw how embarrassed the poor woman was and before anyone could notice the large red puddle spreading on the table, she intentionally knocked over her own glass of wine and then loudly exclaimed how clumsy she was. Everyone's attention was immediately drawn to the First Lady, and the wait staff hurried to clean the table. The woman recovered and when she realized what had happened, she was forever grateful for the First Lady's act of kindness.

One of Eleanor Roosevelt's most famous quotes was, "No one can make you feel inferior without your consent." Although she was a brilliant individual and one of the most influential women in American history, she actually had to overcome significant self-esteem issues that stemmed from a difficult childhood. Orphaned at a young age, she was raised by a grandmother who constantly criticized her looks.[18] She grew up thinking she was unattractive and was very shy until she met and married Franklin Delano Roosevelt.

As his political career started to take off, she bloomed as well and found strength in supporting the troops and those at home during World War I. When FDR became president, she took advantage of her position as First Lady and became a champion of women's rights, racial equality and many different charitable organizations. All of these things built up her confidence, which allowed her to do even more good works. Later in life, she was appointed to the United Nations and was even encouraged to run for president herself. Her dedication to helping others continues to inspire men and women today.

Like Eleanor Roosevelt when she was younger, some of us may lack a healthy sense of self worth or may not be comfortable with who we are. But we can cultivate self-confidence and inner strength by learning how to be more giving and selfless whenever we can. When we make a conscious effort to be a better person, not perfect, just better — we start to see ourselves in a positive light. We feel good about ourselves, which in turn boosts our self-esteem. With time and ongoing effort, we will feel stronger, more confident and can slowly overcome our fear of saying or doing the wrong thing. Likewise, any action or comment that was directed toward us and meant to be hurtful ends up losing its sting when we know that we are doing our best to follow the right path. It's almost like having an invisible shield.

But the best part of having inner strength is when we share it. Like the flame of a candle that is used to light others, our strength does not diminish regardless of how many people we share it with. The flame continues to burn just as brightly, and with the light of the other candles it can brilliantly illuminate a room that was once dark.

I saw this for myself recently in an elevator of all places. An old Navy friend of mine who is a pediatric neurologist from Virginia was in Cleveland for a speaking engagement and dropped by my hospital to say hello. As my clinic schedule was full that day, I didn't have time to take him off campus for lunch so we went to the restaurant inside the hotel that's attached to the hospital.

The hotel itself is rather upscale and a bit expensive. Some patients and their families stay there when they have clinic appointments, but the hotel's clientele consists largely of VIPs and businesspeople who attend meetings in the hotel's conference rooms. That day I was dressed in my usual work attire of a skirt and sweater, but my friend who couldn't care less about appearances was wearing jeans and a University of Virginia sweatshirt. While waiting for the hotel elevator, we stood next to a group of stern-looking businessmen in dark suits. When the doors opened, we all filed in and crammed ourselves into the tight space. Just as the doors were about to close, a middle-aged woman in jeans and a faded sweatshirt managed to squeeze in at the last minute, causing the elevator doors to open and close again. The woman apologized for holding us up and looked at all of the businessmen on the elevator. No one said a word, but when she saw my friend she turned to him and said quietly, "I think we're underdressed."

Always the super-friendly guy who can make small talk with a telephone pole, my friend got this giant grin on his face and said in faux horror, "We ARE underdressed. No one told me about the board meeting in the elevator today. I definitely would have worn a suit if I'd known." Everyone started laughing and as the doors opened up on our floor a few moments later, one of the businessmen said that he loved Virginia's football team so my friend was dressed just fine according to him. With his wonderful sense of humor and natural self-confidence, my friend lit up the entire elevator. What had been a slightly tense atmosphere was now filled with joy and a shared sense of humanity. It was funny, heart-warming, and makes for a wonderful memory that I will always cherish. This is what happens when we refuse to be defined by what others think of us, when we can draw from our inner strength and see the enormity of the world beyond Main Street.

The Stories We Tell

D riving is the perfect time to practice mindfulness meditation. When I drive, I usually don't listen to the radio or talk on the phone, and I certainly don't try to text anyone. But once in a while, especially on a long road trip or after a stressful day at work, I'll turn on the radio just to get out of my head. On those occasions, I often find myself subconsciously scanning the song lyrics for meaning or a morsel of truth that will make me a better person, happier or just not as stressed. One afternoon while I was flipping through stations, I heard the same phrase twice within a few hours. The first was from a song I'd never heard before, and the second was in an interview with a writer who'd just finished a novel. Both said variations of the same thing: we are here but for a short while.

It's certainly not a new sentiment, but given that I heard it on the radio twice in one afternoon it definitely caught my attention. It reminded me of a scene in the movie *Before Midnight* where one of the characters, an older woman who'd been recently widowed, talked about how our time here is so fleeting and that we are all just passing through.[19] It wasn't said in a morbid sense, nor was it an announcement of our mortality in which she was marking our existence with a definitive beginning and end. It felt deeper. It was more like a reference to the transient nature of the human condition, that we may be as ancient Buddhist teachings described, "a flash of lightning in a summer cloud."[20] We come and we go. Yet we create so much drama while we're here. Or we get distracted from the things that really matter. And if purifying our minds so that we can return to a state of grace is one of the reasons for our existence, then really we have very little time at all. Not only that, but many of our goals are so wrong, so misguided that we can easily stray from the path and become lost for years.

Life is hard to be sure. In the words of my patient with multiple sclerosis who does the best she can despite of all of her disabilities, life doesn't stop because we want it to. Our time here is so short that no matter what happens to us or how painful our life is, we have to get up and keep going. Every day we have a choice. Maybe we can't change our bodies, our families, our jobs or our living situation. But we can choose what story we want to tell ourselves, because that's what we have. That's the only thing we can really control. Our story.

There are some psychologists and philosophers who believe that the concept of the self is simply one big story, that we are composed of nothing more than a body and a narrative. On one level this may be true. We each have our own narrative that's formed by a collection of memories, thoughts and emotions that we keep with us and add to as time goes on. But confining our existence to that of a mere narrative doesn't fully capture us as living, breathing human beings, because of the fact that we continue to exist even if we lose all of the stories of our past, like people who have suffered from a stroke, amnesia, or dementia. Their memories may have faded with disease, but they continue to think and feel and experience life as each minute passes, all the while creating new stories.

With each new experience, even if it's just the sensation of something touching our skin, the chemistry of the brain changes. This can be seen on special MRIs that show how different parts of the brain light up as our neuronal circuits start firing in unique patterns depending on what we say, do and think. This variation of brain function in response to our thoughts and experiences extends to the inner workings of the mind in that the stories we tell ourselves are also constantly evolving depending on what happens to us from moment to moment. And that's where we can make a difference. We can change those stories ourselves.

This is not to say that we should be delusional or intentionally misrepresent ourselves. Facts are facts, and we can't change what actually happened in the past. If our parents divorced, if we lost a loved one, if we took a wrong turn somewhere in life, then those facts stand. But as we all know, a story is more than just facts. It includes so many other details, such as the perspective we had, our level of maturity and the emotional reactions we experienced at the time. It's also dependent on the input of other people who were there with us, and how accurately we end up remembering everything. As the months and years go by, our stories are further shaped by our education, life experiences and personal reflections. They're continuously changing within our own minds whether we want them to or not. Even when every effort is made to be as truthful and objective as possible, two people who witnessed the same event at the same time can remember completely different things.

Years ago, two of my friends who are both neurologists witnessed a terrible shooting in which a woman and her lover were shot in front of a building by her estranged husband. The woman was killed, but her lover managed to escape into the building with the husband chasing after him still holding the gun. My two friends were sitting in the building when the lover and the husband literally ran right past them. Shortly afterward, when the police asked them to describe the two people they saw, one friend said it was two white guys, and the other said it was two black guys. They were both wrong. The lover was Hispanic and the husband was African-American. Neither of my friends had intended to deceive anyone, but that's how they remembered or rather misremembered it.

Stories no doubt change with time. And some of them should. Again, it's not the facts that should be altered, but the commentary that we add to them. It's much easier to remember all the negative things from our past, memories of when someone hurt us or of the things we did to hurt others. Guilt, anger, regret, and fear all linger in our memories long after everything has been said and done. And they only grow stronger each time we tell ourselves those painful stories from our past. My mother once told me that when we're in our 20s, any bad experience from childhood or adolescence is simply ignored, because that's when we are starting to explore the world as an adult free to do what we want for the first time in our young lives. Then in our 30s, we are too busy with our careers and starting our families to notice anything beyond what is happening right in front of us. But then in our 40s, life quiets down a bit or at least stabilizes, and the memories that we've kept just beneath the surface start to creep back into the conscious mind. We start to feel restless and anxious, or experience unexplained depression, sadness, anger or all of the above. There is a growing sense of dissatisfaction that arises from within and affects how we interact with the people around us, especially those that we love. It is then that things can start to unravel if we don't face up to our past.

The painful experiences of youth tend to be the most powerful and can affect us years later. But as everyone knows, bad things can happen at any time resulting in the creation of new stories that are not in the least bit positive. When a man's wife left him for someone else, he felt there was something wrong with him and for a while convinced himself that he would never be good enough for anyone else to love ever again. He went through a very difficult period and ended up going through counseling to stop all the negative feedback he was generating himself. When a woman attorney was let go after her firm in New York went through some major downsizing, she had a hard time finding a new job and was turned down by one firm after another despite an Ivy League education and years of experience. At one point, she stopped sending out her resume because she thought she'd just be ignored or rejected again. Only when her friends convinced her to move back to California and gave her support and encouragement was she able to get back to the job search again with some degree of confidence.

We all have to let go of these stories. Some of them are destructive while others are just wrong. Our memories can fail us and we end up adding things to our story that never happened, forgetting important details or getting things completely mixed up, like my friends who turned out to be rather poor witnesses to a murder. Our stories can also be skewed by depression, poor self-esteem and other negative experiences that distort the lens by which we view our past, present and future. As inaccurate as they may be, we continue to carry these stories with us believing that they define who we are.

The reality though is that we are not merely the sum of our experiences. We are so much more than just a collection of stories. As living beings with free will and the ability to form new thoughts and ideas, our minds are capable of anything. We have the power to change our stories at any time by adding to them a new level of understanding and forgiveness, which allows us to let go of our old stories and start our lives anew. Like the lotus flower that emerges from the mud with its soft purple blooms rising above the water, we too can learn to bloom again.

Acknowledgments

This book would not have been possible without the wonderful stories that my friends, family and patients have shared with me over the years. For my Dad, my brother Winston and his family (Karmyn, Dean and Clark), thank you for being a continuous source of love and encouragement. For Glen Stevens, Rich Schlenk, Richard Ransohoff, Mike Strunc, Angela Ting, Yarixa Barillas, Steven and Owen Shook, thank you so much for your friendship and for letting me share your stories.

A special thanks to Kim Woodward for your invaluable editorial help. Also, thank you Mary Bruce Rae-Grant and Rob Patrick for your early read of the manuscript.

For Judy Lee, Alexandra Villa-Forte, Narumol Taweesedt (my dear Aunt Meow), Aimee Bergant, Ngamchit Phatoommas, Patrick and Maureen Sweeney, as always thank you for your support.

Most importantly, I am deeply grateful to my mother. Thank you, Sifu, for listening to my stories. I know that many of them are just variations of the same story with the same punchline, but you always listen with patience and kindness. Thank you for being my teacher, my life coach and my inspiration. You will always be a star in my eyes.

REFERENCES

[1] Alm, David "An Elite State Of Mind." *Running Times* March 4, 2013. Retrieved from http://www.runnersworld.com/race-training/elite-state-mind on October 19, 2014.

[2] *Annie Hall*. Dir. Woody Allen. Perfs. Diane Keaton, Woody Allen. Rollins-Joffe Productions, 1977.

[3] Carnegie, Dale. *How to Win Friends and Influence People*. New York: Simon Schuster, 1936.

[4] Frost, Robert. *A Servant to Servants.* North of Boston 1914. Retrieved from http://www.gutenberg.org/ebooks/3026 on March 30, 2015.

[5] Frankl, Viktor. *Man's Search for Meaning*. Boston: Beacon Press, 2006.

[6] Wallace, David Foster. *Infinite Jest*. New York: Little Brown, 1996.

[7] *Maleficent*. Dir. Robert Stromberg. Perfs. Angelina Jolie, Elle Fanning. Walt Disney Pictures & Roth Films, 2014.

[8] Williams, Tennessee. *A Streetcar Named Desire*. New York: New American Library, 1990.

[9] Chang, Iris. *The Rape of Nanking: The Forgotten Holocaust of World War II*. New York: Penguin Books, 1998.

[10] *Up in the Air*. Dir. Jason Reitman. Perfs. George Clooney, Vera Farmiga. Paramount Pictures, 2009.

[11] Director Jason Reitman Finds His Feet 'Up In The Air.' *All Things Considered*. WCPN, Cleveland. 30 Nov. 2009. Radio.

[12] Brown, Peter and Broeske, Pat H. *Howard Hughes: The Untold Story*. New York: Penguin Books, 1996.

[13] Mother Teresa. *No Greater Love*. Novato: New World Library, 2002.

[14] *The Edge of Tomorrow: Live, Die, Repeat*. Dir. Doug Liman.

Perfs. Tom Cruise, Emily Blunt. Warner Bros. Pictures, 2014.

[15] *Groundhog Day*. Dir. Harold Ramis. Perfs. Bill Murray, Andy McDowell. Columbia Pictures Corp, 1993.

[16] *Pleasantville*. Dir. Gary Ross. Perfs. Tobey Maguire, Reese Witherspoon. New Line Cinema & Larger Than Life Productions, 1998.

[17] Joyce, James. *The Dead*. Dubliners 1914. New York: Norton, 2003.

[18] "Eleanor Roosevelt Biography". *National First Ladies' Library*. Archived from the original on November 21, 2012. Retrieved from http://www.firstladies.org/biographies/firstladies.aspx?biography=33 on February 19, 2015.

[19] *Before Midnight*. Dir. Richard Linklater. Perfs. Julie Delphy, Ethan Hawke. Faliro House Productions, 2013.

[20] Price, A.F., Lam, Wong-Mou. *The Diamond Sutra and the Sutra of Hui-neng*. Boston: Shambhala Publications, 2005.

Also By The Author
A Cup of Salt: Five Steps to Health and Happiness